The Bible and Sexual Violence Against Men

At least 1 in 6 men have experienced some form of sexual violence. *The Bible and Sexual Violence Against Men* argues that the shame and stigma around male sexual abuse are interwoven with contemporary social and cultural concepts of masculinity, and are also found in the ancient world and biblical texts themselves.

This book is interdisciplinary and has three main areas of exploration:

- #MenToo? Exploring the myths around sexual violence against men
- Sexual violence against men in the Hebrew Bible
- Reading Jesus' enforced nudity at the crucifixion as sexual violence.

Given the enduring importance of the Bible in contemporary society, this book explores the biblical texts that depict sexual violence against men. It examines critical approaches from theology, biblical, and religious studies perspectives, while also exploring insights from the fields of sociology, psychology, and criminology as well as referring to legal cases and legislation, charity work, and media-focussed articles. In seeking to serve a number of interested readers, including those who are not familiar with the Bible, short summaries of the biblical texts under discussion are given in each case.

Chris Greenough is Senior Lecturer in Theology and Religion, Edge Hill University, UK.

Rape Culture, Religion and the Bible
Series Editors:
Katie Edwards
University of Sheffield, UK
Caroline Anne Blyth
University of Auckland, New Zealand
Johanna Stiebert
University of Leeds, UK

Rape Myths, the Bible and #MeToo
Johanna Stiebert

Telling Terror in Judges 19
Rape and Reparation for the Levite's Wife
Helen Paynter

Resisting Rape Culture
The Hebrew Bible and Hong Kong Sex Workers
Nany Nan Hoon Tan

The Bible and Sexual Violence Against Men
Chris Greenough

For more information about this series, please visit: www.routledge.com/Rape-Culture-Religion-and-the-Bible/book-series/RCRB

The Bible and Sexual Violence Against Men

Chris Greenough

Routledge
Taylor & Francis Group
LONDON AND NEW YORK

First published 2021
by Routledge
2 Park Square, Milton Park, Abingdon, Oxon OX14 4RN

and by Routledge
605 Third Avenue, New York, NY 10017

First issued in paperback 2022

Routledge is an imprint of the Taylor & Francis Group, an informa business

© 2021 Chris Greenough

The right of Chris Greenough to be identified as author of this work has been asserted by him in accordance with sections 77 and 78 of the Copyright, Designs and Patents Act 1988.

All rights reserved. No part of this book may be reprinted or reproduced or utilised in any form or by any electronic, mechanical, or other means, now known or hereafter invented, including photocopying and recording, or in any information storage or retrieval system, without permission in writing from the publishers.

Trademark notice: Product or corporate names may be trademarks or registered trademarks, and are used only for identification and explanation without intent to infringe.

Publisher's Note
The publisher has gone to great lengths to ensure the quality of this reprint but points out that some imperfections in the original copies may be apparent.

British Library Cataloguing-in-Publication Data
A catalogue record for this book is available from the British Library

Library of Congress Cataloging-in-Publication Data
A catalog record for this book has been requested

ISBN: 978-0-367-56287-8 (pbk)
ISBN: 978-0-367-46557-5 (hbk)
ISBN: 978-1-003-02960-1 (ebk)

DOI: 10.4324/9781003029601

Typeset in Times New Roman
by Apex CoVantage, LLC

*To Caroline Blyth, Katie Edwards, and Johanna Stiebert,
for your inspiration and support.*

Contents

Acknowledgements ix

Introduction 1

1 #MenToo? Myths around sexual abuse against men 8

Introduction 8
Defining sexual abuse against men and male rape 9
Why is there so much shame and stigma about male rape? 12
The impact of abuse and rape on men 15
#Me(n)Too? 16
#ChurchToo 18
The role of religion in obfuscating sexual violence against men 20
The perilous consequences of reading Genesis 19: 1–29 as a condemnation of homosexuality 21
Misogyny and fear of queer 24
Conclusion 27
References 31

2 Sexual violence against men in the Hebrew Bible 34

Introduction 34
Hegemonic masculinity in the Bible 35
Sexual violence against men 39
  Lot and his daughters (Genesis 19: 30–38) 39
  Joseph and Potiphar's wife (Genesis 39) 41

    The attempted gang rape of men (Genesis 19: 1–29;
        Judges 19) 44
    Metaphorical enactments of sexual violence
      against men 47
      Noah, Ham, and the curse of Caanan
        (Genesis 9: 20–27) 47
      Ehud and Eglon (Judges 3: 12–30) 49
      Jael and Sisera (Judges 4) 51
      Samson and Delilah (Judges 16) 52
      Further examples 55
    Conclusion 56
    References 59

3   Jesus too?   62

    Introduction 62
    'Behold the man' (John 19: 5) 62
    #JesusToo? 68
    Problematics in representing Jesus' sex and sexuality 70
    The divine penis: purity, power, potency 75
    Textual violations? 79
    Conclusion 81
    References 84

Afterword   87
Index of biblical passages   90
Index of authors and subjects   93

Acknowledgements

The impetus to write this book comes from my own personal drive to ensure that my academic research engages with contemporary issues: namely that the study of religion, biblical studies, and theology matters to people today. My work seeks to advocate for marginalised and silenced voices. This drive continues to be fuelled by brilliant friends and my wonderful family. Thanks to colleagues at Edge Hill University, especially Allison Moore, who cheered me to the finish line, and to my students, who engage enthusiastically and offer their own insights when I teach about my research.

I am grateful to Rebecca Shillabeer, senior editor at Routledge, for commissioning this book, as well as the support from Amy Doffegnies, editorial assistant.

The idea for this book stems from a professional and personal friendship with Katie Edwards, who has discussed and shared ideas with me throughout, as well as being an invaluable source of encouragement, support, and hilarious text messages. Thanks are also due to Johanna Stiebert, who commented on a very early draft of Chapter 3 and read through the manuscript, and has provided good-humoured inspiration during the course of the book's journey. Endless thanks to Caroline Blyth, who read drafts of the manuscript and offered (copious!) critical insights and feedback that has undoubtedly enriched the contents of these pages. As directors of the Shiloh Project and editors of the series 'Rape Culture, Religion and the Bible', the support I have received from these three strong, wonderful academics and friends will remain with me throughout my career. Of course, any faults or errors are entirely my own.

Final thanks to my fabulous partner, Mark Edward, for your love, encouragement, reassurance, and humour.

Introduction

The most prolific case of serial rape in UK legal history involved the rape of nearly 200 men. Here, I choose not to name the perpetrator, given that some criminals have aspirations of notoriety and desire publicity. The perpetrator, a 36-year-old Indonesian man, was found guilty of drugging, raping, and sexually assaulting 48 men in Manchester, UK. But police estimate that there were at least 190 victims, as the perpetrator collected evidence of his assaults by filming them on his mobile phones. Across his two phones, there were over 800 videos of men being raped or sexually assaulted. Police had to use this evidence to approach men they subsequently identified as victims, many of whom were unaware of what had happened to them. The majority of victims were drunk or drugged, often blacking out for the duration of the time of their assault. One of the methods the perpetrator used to entice victims was to offer them support while they were feeling inebriated. The perpetrator described himself to them as a 'Good Samaritan', identifying himself as Christian and taking them to his flat under the pretext of providing care and shelter. The vast majority of victims were heterosexual men.[1]

At least 1 in 6 men have experienced some form of sexual violence.[2] Within rape culture, there exist a number of myths that become obstacles to understanding, recognising, and labelling sexual abuse. Some of the most common myths around sexual violence against men include: men cannot be sexually violated; a man is blameworthy or gains pleasure from the experience; sexual abuse is less damaging and harmful to male victims than female victims. There is also a mythical association between sexual violence and homosexuality: only gay men sexually abuse other men, or being a victim of sexual abuse makes you gay. These myths, therefore, need to be countered with facts. Boys and men can be and are victims of sexual assault, and this has nothing to do with their masculinity or sexual or gender identities. Boys and men may have different experiences and responses to their abuse than girls or women, but that does not make the abuse any less harmful. Sexual abuse against boys or men is not always perpetrated by other men, but girls and women can be perpetrators. And no one, regardless of their gender identity or sexuality, is to blame for their own assault.

What does the Bible have to do with sexual violence against men? The Bible is a text which holds central importance in the faith traditions of Judaism and Christianity. Aside from its function in religious life, it holds a certain import in public life, too; people 'swear on the Bible', in common parlance, and literally swear oaths to truth-telling in court and legal settings. John Barton notes how 'this does not necessarily mean that people read the Bible very much: it is an icon rather than an object of study' (2019: 6). Given its leverage as a cultural icon, people are often shocked to learn that the Bible contains lengthy accounts of violence in both of its testaments. Biblical scholar David Clines observes how 'on average, there are more than six instances of violence on every page of the Hebrew Bible, including more than one of divine violence' (2018: 3). There are passages that narrate harrowing and shocking experiences, including war, murder, and sexual violence.

In general, critical studies into sexual violence experienced by men remain relatively scarce compared to scholarship exploring the rape and sexual violation of women. This is undoubtedly due to the fact that women experience sexual violence on a much greater scale than men. The flourishing critical examination of the Bible, religion, and rape culture can be seen as a response to the urgent need of such scholarship in contemporary contexts. It would be highly misleading to attribute this surge in scholarship to the #MeToo movement, as feminist biblical scholars have been exploring rape culture for quite some time. Phyllis Trible's influential book, *Texts of Terror: Literary Feminist Readings of Biblical Narratives* (1984), explores the tragic stories of four women in the Hebrew Bible who were subjected to terrible violence: Hagar, Tamar, an unnamed concubine, and the daughter of Jephthah. J. Cheryl Exum resists traditional androcentric readings of scripture and instead goes in search of the fragmented texts of women's stories in *Fragmented Women: Feminist Subversions of Biblical Narratives* (1993; reprinted 2016). Caroline Blyth explores the sexual violation of Dinah in *The Narrative of Rape in Genesis 34: Interpreting Dinah's Silence* (2010). Likewise, Susanne Scholz's *Sacred Witness: Rape in the Hebrew Bible* (2010) critically confronts biblical stories of rape. Feminist concerns with men and masculinity too have been incorporated in the scholarship into rape culture and the Bible. Exum (2016 [1993]) and Scholz (2010) both provide detailed examination of attempted male rape or instances where sexual violence against men is alluded to, alongside their comprehensive accounts of female rape in the Bible. More recently, and in light of #MeToo, we see the publication of a three-volume series exploring interdisciplinary, biblical, and Christian perspectives, entitled *Rape Culture, Gender Violence, and Religion* (2018, Blyth, Colgan, and Edwards, eds), and Johanna Stiebert's *Rape Myths, the Bible, and #MeToo* (2019a).

To my knowledge, *The Bible and Sexual Violence Against Men* is the first book dedicated exclusively to an exploration of sexual violence against men and the Bible. The principal aim of this book is to explore the interdisciplinary intersections between the Bible and religious, cultural, and social contexts in which sexual violence is perpetrated against men. This book is wholly interdisciplinary. In addition to utilising and critically examining approaches to the themes from theology, biblical, and religious studies perspectives, I explore texts from the fields of sociology, psychology, and criminology as well as referring to legal cases and legislation, charity work, and media-focussed articles. This allows for a holistic and original reading of the Bible and sexual violence against men in contemporary contexts. In seeking to serve a number of interested readers, including those who are not familiar with the Bible, I offer short summaries of the biblical texts under discussion in each case to elucidate my arguments. For readers who approach this text from their own faith perspectives and backgrounds, and/or who may be sceptical about my approach to the Bible here, I urge them to share the same commitment to social justice as is etched on these pages. Ronald Long makes a helpful point to bear in mind:

> One would therefore expect that those who consider themselves among the faithful would be on the forefront of movements for social justice, especially since every Passover the Jew would remember what it would be like to be a slave in the household of Egypt, and the Christian would remember that his or her Lord was executed as an expendable historical no-account.
>
> (2006: 1)

One charge levied at work such as this would be the accusation that it commits the inexcusable sin of anachronism in biblical studies: that my readings of the biblical texts move away from the authors' original intentions or ancient contexts in which they were written. As will become clear, I argue that the shame and stigma around male nudity and sexual violence against men are interwoven with contemporary social and cultural concepts of masculinity and are also found in the ancient world and biblical texts themselves. Moreover, I am less concerned with speculating on authorial intentions or anticipated meanings, but I follow scholars such as Katie Edwards, Caroline Blyth, and Johanna Stiebert who research and write on the topic of rape culture and the Bible and are more interested in how the

Bible functions, operates, and holds status and an authority of its own in the contemporary world in which we live. Following Stiebert (2019b), my work here explores 'rape culture readings [that] seek to navigate between the world of the biblical text and a discrete contemporary context' (2019b: 73). Or, as Edwards states:

> We do not have and cannot retrieve authorial intention for the biblical text, but what we do have is the way the text functions right now, in front of eyes, and the meanings, messages and implicit social and cultural assumptions it is used to convey.
>
> (2010: ix)

Likewise, Blyth observes how biblical texts reflect the attitudes, contexts, and experiences of the communities in which they were written, but she highlights how 'they have the potential to validate and endorse these same ideologies, values, and assumptions within the communities in which they are read' (2010: 7).

The Bible is a book that is unequivocally androcentric; it is a man's book, where men are largely the protagonists and the readers are assumed to be male. Yet, as this book argues, patriarchy and heteronormativity serve as foundations for hegemonic masculinity, which is damaging not only to women, but also to men. Therefore, my focus on reading and interpreting biblical narratives depicting sexual violence against men is concerned with highlighting this harmful impact of patriarchy and hegemonic masculinity on men themselves. Male gender performativity and social expectations of 'real' men are so historically and culturally ingrained that we can trace back examples in the Bible itself. Toxic masculinity, generated through patriarchy, heteronormativity, and misogyny, is at play in the Bible. The central thesis of this book is that in the Bible and in contemporary contexts, ideas and ideals of masculinity lead to a blindness to male rape and sexual violence against men; they uphold dangerous myths about gendered violence.

Before I set out the structure of the book, I wish to offer a note about terminology. In the book, I use the term 'sexual abuse' as a generic category to denote any unwanted or forced sexual activity, but it also includes non-physical manipulation or exploitation, such as grooming. My use of the term 'abuse' is not intended to lessen the impact of sexual violence, and it is often used alongside the words 'assault', 'rape', and 'violence' in reference to particular crimes.

The book is organised into three chapters. Chapter 1 has two main foci. The first is concerned with defining sexual abuse and exploring the myths around sexual violence against men. In my exploration of shame and stigma, I examine the impact of abuse and rape on men from psychological and sociological perspectives. Given the popularity of the #MeToo movement, I consider how attempts from men to label their own abuse on social media have sometimes been seen as a co-opting intrusion into feminist spaces. This, in turn, raises questions about the support and spaces afforded to male victims. The second area of focus in Chapter 1 discusses the role of religion in obfuscating sexual violence against men. My argument here is that religion, with its legacy of patriarchy, heteronormativity, and misogyny, has served to fuel unhelpful and unrealistic expectations of masculinities for men. One obvious example of this is in the traditional interpretation of the biblical story of Sodom and Gomorrah (Genesis 19: 1–29), which is viewed as God's condemnation and punishment for homosexual intentions. This is a 'clobber text', used to justify homophobic and homonegative attitudes in religious traditions. For a man to take the place of a woman, whether through consensual sexual activity or through sexual violence, is degrading on either account according to religious teachings, as he would be assuming a lesser position: that of a woman. What becomes apparent in my examination of this text is that traditional religious unease around homosexuality is undoubtedly linked to misogyny.

In Chapter 2, attention turns to the Hebrew Bible specifically. It opens with an explanatory tour of masculinity in the Bible. Following on from this, my discussion of sexual violence is also bipartite. The first part examines what can be read as actual cases of sexual violence against men. Here, the reader will find discussion on the following texts: Lot's daughters getting him drunk and forcing him to have sex with them in order to procreate (Genesis 19: 30–38); Joseph's resistance of the sexual advances of Potiphar's wife and the false allegations she makes against him (Genesis 39); and the attempted gang rape of men by other men (Genesis 19: 1–29; Judges 19). Bearing in mind Exum's assertion that 'homosexual rape is too threatening to narrate' (2016 [1993]: 146), I move on from more obvious accounts of sexual violence against men to explore some metaphorical enactments. Here, I offer examples found in the following biblical passages: Noah, Ham, and the Curse of Caanan (Genesis 9: 20–27); Ehud and Eglon (Judges 3: 12–30); Jael and Sisera (Judges 4); and Samson and Delilah (Judges 16).

Chapter 3 confronts one issue which is of central importance when exploring sexual violence against men in the Bible: the stripping of Jesus at his crucifixion in the New Testament. Here, I examine sources that denote how such an act was a public humiliation and shaming of a man. Reading Jesus as a victim of sexual violence remains a contentious issue in theology and biblical studies, as well as in wider faith communities. Accordingly, I explore the reason for some of the controversy surrounding this through the limited, but emerging, scholarship in this area. I examine representations of Jesus in art and theology that are deemed taboo, including the unlikelihood of Jesus being afforded a loin cloth at the crucifixion, which has served to cover up his modesty in art depictions for over two millennia. The same representation has also hidden the nature of his abuse as sexual. The discussion then focusses on the masculinity and sexuality of Jesus, noting how this is wrapped up in notions of purity, power, and potency. The chapter concludes with my argument that a blindness to the sexual violence Jesus endured has led to a blindness to sexual violence against men in general. The short concluding section of the book considers the impact and issues of exploring religion, rape culture, and the Bible in public settings and in higher education.

Notes

1 Helen Pidd, 'How Serial Rapist Posed as a Good Samaritan to Lure Victims', *The Guardian*, 06 January 2020. Available: www.theguardian.com/uk-news/2020/jan/06/reynhard-sinaga-serial-rapist-posed-good-samaritan-lure-men.
2 '1 in 6'. Available: https://1in6.org/.

References

Barton, John. 2019. *A History of the Bible: The Book and Its Faiths*. London: Penguin Books.
Blyth, Caroline. 2010. *The Narrative of Rape in Genesis 34: Interpreting Dinah's Silence*. Oxford: Oxford University Press.
Blyth, Caroline, Emily Colgan and Katie B. Edward. 2018a. *Rape Culture, Gender Violence, and Religion: Biblical Perspectives*. Cham: Palgrave Macmillan.
Blyth, Caroline, Emily Colgan and Katie B. Edward. 2018b. *Rape Culture, Gender Violence, and Religion: Christian Perspectives*. Cham: Palgrave Macmillan.
Blyth, Caroline, Emily Colgan and Katie B. Edward. 2018c. *Rape Culture, Gender Violence, and Religion: Interdisciplinary Perspectives*. Cham: Palgrave Macmillan.
Clines, David. 2018. 'The Ubiquitous Language of Violence in the Hebrew Bible'. Paper presented at the Joint Meeting of Oudtestamentisch Werkgezelschap, Society for Old Testament Studies, and Old Testament Society of South Africa, Groningen, The Netherlands, 22 August 2019. Available: www.academia.edu/37260426/The_Ubiquitous_Language_of_Violence_in_the_Hebrew_Bible.
Edwards, Katie. 2010. *Admen and Eve. The Bible in Contemporary Advertising*. Sheffield: Sheffield Phoenix Press.
Exum, J. Cheryl. 2016 [1993]. *Fragmented Women: Feminist Subversions of Biblical Narratives*. Second Edition. London: Bloomsbury.
Long, Ronald E. 2006. 'Introduction. Disarming Biblically Based Gay-Bashing'. In *The Queer Bible Commentary*. Edited by Deryn Guest, Robert E. Goss, Mona West and Thomas Bohache. London: SCM Press, pp. 1–18.

Scholz, Susanne. 2010. *Sacred Witness: Rape in the Hebrew Bible*. Minneapolis: Fortress Press.
Stiebert, Johanna. 2019a. *Rape Myths, the Bible and #MeToo*. London: Routledge.
Stiebert, Johanna. 2019b. 'The Wife of Potiphar, Sexual Harassment, and False Rape Allegation'. In *The Bible and Gender Troubles in Africa*. Edited by Joachim Kügler, Rosinah Gabaitse and Johanna Stiebert. Bamberg: University of Bamberg Press, pp. 73–114.

1 #MenToo? Myths around sexual abuse against men

Introduction

This chapter problematises the myths surrounding sexual violence against men and how they are intricately intertwined with ideas and ideals of hegemonic masculinity. Hegemonic masculinity is a practice that gives status and authority to a man's dominant position in society, to the exclusion of women and other marginalised masculinities, including bisexual and gay men, and queer or transgender people. Raewyn Connell's extensive contributions to the study of hegemonic masculinity demonstrate how it is socially, culturally, and politically institutionalised and regulated by ridicule, intimidation, and violence (1995). Hegemonic masculinity creates social rules by which men are expected to perform masculinity in particular ways; men who fall foul of these standards are subsequently emasculated. There is, therefore, an immediate connection between patriarchy and hegemonic masculinity; as Connell states, 'men's interest in patriarchy is condensed in hegemonic masculinity and is defended by all the cultural machinery that exalts hegemonic masculinity' (1995: 241).

Accordingly, this chapter explores how religion is part of the cultural machinery of hegemonic masculinity, as Judaism and Christianity have found authority for patriarchy in the scriptural texts. This has served to bolster myths around sexual violence against men. First, I define and contextualise sexual abuse against men and male rape in contemporary society and culture. This allows for a critical examination of the impact of abuse and rape on men, including the notions of silence, stigma, shame, and post-traumatic stress disorder, as well as other physical and emotional consequences. This provides a necessary background to document how hegemonic masculinity is equally toxic to men as well as women and serves to perpetuate myths around sexual violence against men. Next, I explore how the #MeToo movement on social media provided an extended platform for men to share their own experiences of abuse, though this was met with criticism about men sabotaging what was originally understood to be a feminist space. Yet, the focus on #Me(n)Too challenges the myths around sexual abuse against men and offers a platform for male survivors to share their stories, thereby providing a counter-narrative to hegemonic masculinity. Moving away from social media to the church itself, the following section focusses on the church as an institution steeped in patriarchy and hegemonic masculinity, and the #ChurchToo movement offered a further platform for sexual abuse against male survivors to be recognised. The final section of this chapter explores the role of religion in obfuscating sexual abuse against men. I argue how homonegative pronouncements and doctrines from churches have conflated sexual abuse against men with same-sex attraction through a legacy of misinterpretations of the scriptural texts (Genesis 19: 1–29; Judges 19), thereby demonising both homosexuality and male rape as if they were the same. The false association of male rape with homosexuality has been problematic in terms of victims actually reporting their assault. This also raises the question of support for men who are victims of sexual violence, but especially for gay and bisexual men who have long been considered deviant to the regulation of heterosexuality, and therefore their abuse is equated with such deviancy.

Defining sexual abuse against men and male rape

There is undeniably a culture of stigma associated with sexual abuse against men. According to the charity '1 in 6', at least 1 in 6 men are sexually abused or assaulted during their lifetime. The charity uses this statistic to denote men's 'unwanted sexual experiences', observing how many men do not want or are not ready to label such experiences as sexual abuse or assault. The organisation originally started with the objective of offering support to men who had unwanted sexual experiences in childhood, but now encompasses support for those who have also been victimised as adults.[1]

In UK legislation, the Sex Offences Act (2003) describes rape as penetration with a penis, vaginally or anally, without consent.[2] A person convicted of rape faces imprisonment of up to a life sentence.[3] Therefore, in legal terms, only those with a penis can be designated as rapists. However, assault by penetration, which may include an object or anything other than a penis, does hold the same potential sentence of life imprisonment. The semantic connection between the word 'penetration' and 'penis' serves linguistically to denote that the focus seems to be on men raping other men. Whereas statistics pertaining to male rape centre on the anal penetration of the victim, what does not constitute male rape, legally, is forcing a man to penetrate another person: a scenario in which the penetrator is actually the victim. Rather, this latter crime falls under the category of 'causing a person to engage in sexual activity without consent' and holds a maximum prison sentence of ten years.[4] Legislation in this area thus reflects and fuels the myths around sexual violence against men, particularly the belief that a man cannot be (technically and legally) raped by a woman, even if there are unwanted sexual advances on his penis.[5] Legislation aside, however, researchers and advocates do describe such an act as male rape due to the lack of consent on the part of the victim.

Of course, ideations of shame and stigma surrounding male sexual assault are so prevalent that accurate data on sexual violence against men is hard to garner, as many boys and men are reluctant to report their assault.[6] Data from the Crime Survey for England and Wales (2018)[7] reveal that 3.8% of men and 20.3% of women have experienced sexual assault since the age of 16. For men specifically, 0.3% experience rape, while the majority of offences (3.7%) were related to unwanted touching or sexual exposure.[8] Information and statistics from the National Sexual Violence Resource Center (NSVRC) in the United States report similar figures; 1 in 6 boys and 1 in 4 girls will experience sexual assault before adulthood.[9] Moreover, 1 in 5 women and 1 in 71 men will be raped at some point in their lives, while 1 in 45 men will be forced to penetrate a partner during their lifetime. Further statistics from the NSVRC show that gay and bisexual men are around twice as likely as heterosexual men to be victims of sexually violent acts other than rape during their lifetime.[10] And, as noted already, these figures are likely to underestimate cases of sexual abuse against men owing to high rates of non-reporting, especially given the double stigma gay and bisexual men face both as victims and because of their sexuality.

One of the myths around sexual violence against men is the false equation between male rape and homosexuality: men who are victims or men who rape other men are presumed to be gay. The reality is that violent sexual assaults are also committed by heterosexual men against other men (and women) as a demonstration of power, control, and strength. Male rape has nothing to do with same-sex desire. Nor are male rape victims predominantly homosexual men. Samantha Hodge and David Canter (1998) have examined cases of sexual violence against men committed by both homosexual and heterosexual perpetrators. They conclude that 'the myth that male sexual assault is extremely rare and only affects homosexual males can be rightfully challenged' (1998: 239). Aliraza Javaid draws a similar conclusion, stating that 'documented research confirms that men do rape other men as a way to boost, preserve and execute "hegemonic masculinity"; that is, the male sexual offender seeks power and control over their subordinate, powerless victim' (2016: 284). This is echoed by A. Nicholas Groth and Ann Burgess (1980), who describe such an act as one which, through the emasculation of the victim, an enhanced sense of dominant masculinity may be evoked for the offender.

Male–male rape is therefore surrounded in taboo and, consequently, silence. Sandesh Sivakumaran highlights that it has not received much attention either in research or in the public conscience as it is 'a cause without a voice' (2005: 1280). He describes how male–male rape is 'tainted' by homophobia and society's unwillingness to give attention to sexual acts between two men, whether desired or unwanted. Recently, Javaid has conducted extensive work in the area of male rape (2016, 2019), as well as focussing on gay male rape (2017). He notes that female rape has, rightly, been given significant attention in sociological and criminological spheres, but the lack of research about male rape demonstrates that it is still surrounded by taboo. This taboo, Javaid argues, reinforces hegemonic masculinity and patriarchal power relations (2016). He states that the silence surrounding sexual assault against men (perpetrated by either men or women) is part of a wider strategy aimed at keeping a man's masculinity intact:

> the act of rape emasculates men, they can at the same time remain silent to prevent their masculinity from being questioned by societies, the police, and the criminal justice system. This form of masculine conduct could keep gay male rape victims' masculinities intact, which arguably can help one to explain and understand their silence.
> (Javaid, 2017: 281)

With the exception of a relatively small number of scholars such as Sivakumaran (2005), Graham (2006), Abdullah-Khan (2008), Weiss (2010), Coxell and King (2010), and Javaid (2016, 2017, 2018, 2019), the lack of social attention to sexual violence against men is also mirrored in academia. Research in the area of male rape initially focussed on prison settings and then began to explore gay male rape (Eigenberg, 1989; Knowles, 1999; Javaid, 2016, 2017). There are still lacunae in the research pertaining to wider issues around female–male rape, male–male rape and female–female rape (Sivakumaran, 2005). The dearth of research in these areas attests to the widespread myths and misunderstandings about men as sexual violence victims, as well as a lack of attention to same-sex acts of sexual violence. Ruth Graham notes how 'the academic discourse on male rape must necessarily construct male bodies as violable and subject to sexual harm' (2006: 188). In this sense, hegemonic masculinity engineers a reluctance to admit male vulnerability. According to Graham, the myths, stigma, and shame associated with sexual abuse have begun to receive greater attention in social research, and there have been attempts to undo some of the misperceptions that sustain rape culture. However, she notes, 'those discussing male rape in the present may be repeating theoretical mistakes that have already been made by those who discuss the sexual assault of women' (2006: 192). These mistakes include seeing men as unexpected and exceptional victims given that sexual assault is a highly gendered crime, alongside limited and misleading definitions of rape and heteronormative assumptions about sexuality. Within the area of biblical studies, feminist scholars have been redressing the mistakes made by traditional biblical interpretation that has silenced the victims. While much feminist scholarship on gender violence in the Bible has focussed on the rape and sexual abuse of women, scholars have started to look at the texts relating attempted male rape more frequently, particularly in recent years (Stiebert, 2019a; Harding, 2018; Exum, 2016 [1993]; Scholz, 2010); this will be further explored in Chapter 2.

Why is there so much shame and stigma about male rape?

According to bell hooks (2000), men's emancipation is part of feminism, as men are also harmed by normative gender roles and patriarchy. The dominant culture of masculinity sets out very narrowly defined social and cultural expectations of being a boy or man. The rules for being a man are learnt from a very early age, then are enforced and regulated through bullying and shame. In *The Little #MeToo Book for Men* (2018), Mark Greene describes the rules as 'man box culture'. According to Greene, the codes and expectations for men are as follows:

> 'Real men' don't show our emotions.
> 'Real men' are heterosexual, hyper-masculine, and sexually dominant.
> 'Real men' never ask for help.
> 'Real men' always have the last word.
> 'Real men' are providers, never caregivers.
> 'Real men' are economically secure.
> 'Real men' are physically and emotionally tough.
> 'Real men' are sports focused.
>
> (2018: 25)

To be a 'real man' in this context is highly toxic. For 'real men', anything feminine is seen as a sign of weakness. Dominant hegemonic masculinity generates cultures of misogyny and homonegativity through microaggressions, verbal insults and physical abuse perpetrated against those who do not conform.

In exploring the intersections between shame and victimisation in the reporting of sexual abuse against men, Karen Weiss observes a feminisation through social and cultural narratives that surround the status of victim:

> '*Real*' men are not supposed to be victims. In fact, a feminization of victimization is evident in the usage of derogatory labels (e.g., sissies,

pansies, pussies) hurled at boys and young men who are perceived as powerless or, more broadly, as having failed to live up to masculine ideals.

(2010: 290)

Not only are men themselves victims of these highly demanding and normative gender expectations of social masculinities, but they also perpetuate these unhealthy ideals by policing and controlling others to conform to the same expectations. Hegemonic masculinity therefore suppresses men's access to wellbeing, as well as impacting on men's contact, emotional expression, friendships, and relationships. In essence, the economy of being a boy or man results in emotional bankruptcy. Hegemonic masculinity promotes attitudes, behaviours, and regulation within society and culture that all serve to perpetuate notions of men as strong, powerful, warrior-like and, consequently, the opposite of a victim. These ideals are harmful to men just as much as they are to women, resulting in concerns around male mental health, access to emotional support, and the prevention of male suicide.

As already noted briefly in the Introduction, there are a number of myths around sexual violence against men that are generated directly from hegemonic masculine ideals and connect broadly to the psychological problems experienced by male survivors of sexual abuse. The myths directly impact how survivors view themselves and how they experience stigma and shame. Moreover, these myths are widespread, and they prevent men from reporting their assault. Adrian Coxell and Michael King's (2010) study also discusses a number of myths that surround male sexual assault specifically:

> the presence of erection or ejaculation implies consent on behalf of the survivor
> a male who is sexually assaulted by another must be gay or have acted in a gay manner
> a male cannot be forced to have sex against his will
> males are less affected by sexual assaults than females
> males who sexually assault other males must be gay
>
> (2010: 381–382)

Another myth about male rape not mentioned by Coxell and King is that a man who is drunk or under the influence of drugs is at least partly to blame for his own assault (Weiss, 2010).[11]

One of the myths stated earlier is that a man would be unable to reach a stage of arousal during an assault. This myth is embedded in contemporary understandings of male sexuality that centre around a focus on the male erection. The false assumption is that arousal somehow equals consent: that a man would not reach the stage of arousal if he was unwilling to participate in the sexual episode. A man being forced to penetrate someone else may also lead to a concomitant myth that if a man ejaculates during an unwanted sexual episode, he has in some way consented to or enjoyed the experience. Yet erection and ejaculation are known to be physiological responses that can be experienced unwillingly or when a man is under stress.

Myths around sexual violence against men are a major source of shame and stigma for victims. While cases of female rape are significantly higher, Javaid claims, 'male rape seems to contain a higher level of stigma than female rape, serving to normalize the acceptance of female rape while abnormalizing male rape' (2019: 51). According to Weiss (2010), there are three significant cultural narratives that invoke shame in a male victim: disempowerment, emasculation, and exposure. A disempowered victim may blame himself for the abuse, especially if he was in some way intoxicated or helpless; he feels shame for being unable to recognise or act against unwanted sexual advances. An emasculated victim has been put in a passive position, and therefore is understood to have been 'feminised' in some way. He feels humiliation because such an assault is not supposed to happen to 'real' men. Being a victim poses a threat to a man's presentation of himself socially as it ruptures the expectations of hegemonic masculinity. This can result in internal or external homophobic reactions if the perpetrator is male, or a perceived violation of gender codes if the perpetrator is female, as male sexual prowess and potency are called into question if a heterosexual man resists the advances of a woman.

The shame experienced in the aftermath of rape is therefore sexual and social: male victims rupture gender expectations of men and hegemonic masculinity. Sexual assault against men is perceived to be in opposition to hegemonic masculinity (including male sexualities and socially regulated gender expectations). In this way, Weiss notes, 'men who are sexually victimized contradict hegemonic definitions of male sexuality' (2010: 290). In many respects, the victimisation of men is perpetrated by other men. Greene is clear to spell out the consequences for those who try to move away from this 'man box culture'; as he states,

> for the courageous men who push back against man box culture, doing manhood differently can get them ostracized, dumped, shamed, fired, beaten or murdered. . . . It is designed to keep men policing, and bullying, and ultimately, fearing each other.
>
> (2018: 29)

Given the shame associated with such a status, it is hardly surprising that many men are unwilling to disclose their assault or to report it to the police. As Javaid notes, men's experiences of sexual violence are often not taken seriously, by either authorities or wider society. He argues that this 'discourages men from coming forward to report rape and to seek help, while also forcing these victims to remain hidden, to keep silent about their crime, and to suffer in silence' (2017: 288).

In her examination of shame, Weiss (2010) remarks how the consequences of sexual abuse for male victims are exacerbated by feelings of inadequacy and failure in relation to their own masculinities. For Weiss, shame is 'an especially debilitating emotion linked to a person's self-worth and identity. For instance, shame is commonly associated with self-condemnation, powerlessness, feelings of disgrace, failure, and inadequacy' (2010: 286). One of the initial reactions post-assault is that men may struggle to recognise that they have, in fact, been victimised (Hawkins et al., 2019). Myths about sexual violence against men are so widespread and socially entrenched that a victim may struggle to acknowledge their own assault as an act of sexual violence, either personally to himself or publicly to others. The association of male rape with homosexuality also impacts identifying oneself as a victim and reporting one's assault. As Noreen Abdullah-Khan (2008) argues, these myths, along with the associated shame and stigma about being a victim, prevent men from reporting their assault to the police. Moreover, she notes that the police may often ascribe to myths around male rape themselves, rendering them unable or unwilling to deal sensitively and effectively with men who report such abuse.

The impact of abuse and rape on men

There are identifiable difficulties experienced and reported by men after sexual assault. Coxell and King produce a list of problems reported after abusive episodes perpetrated by other men: confusion about sexuality, sexual problems, post-traumatic stress disorder (PTSD), problems forming relationships with men, and suicide (2010). After a sexual assault, a man may feel ambiguous or confused about his sexuality, regardless of his sexuality before the assault. Bisexual or gay men may feel conflict about their sexual identifications following an assault, even when they had accepted and embraced their own sexualities previously. Sexual problems are also reported among men post-assault, and these may relate to sexual function (erection/ejaculation), abstinence from sex, or, conversely, promiscuity. PTSD experiences post-assault can result in flashbacks, mood and sleep disturbances, hyper-alertness, and obsessive behaviours.

The impact of sexual assault also results in problems forming close relationships or experiencing mistrust of other men (Coxell and King, 2010). These problems may be generalised, such as the inability to form or sustain peer relationships; or interactional, including situational fears which may bring flashbacks of the assault and its location. Moreover, the stigma surrounding sexual violence against men deters victims from talking openly about their emotions, feelings, worries, and health, which can result in devastating effects on their mental health, including ideations of suicide.[12] Coxell and King also cite 'other problems' encountered by male sexual assault victims, including 'mood disturbances, depression and insomnia and an attack on masculine identity' (2010: 385–387). They note that the level of violence in the sexual assault has a direct correlation with the severity of the after-effects experienced by a man. Therefore, the impact of the sexual assault on the victims' mental health might deter them from reporting. Also, men who are victims of sexual assault perpetrated by a woman also report sexual problems in the aftermath of the assault.

Much of the emic literature written to support male victims of sexual violence is aimed at those who were abused as children, thereby falling into the broader category of 'child sexual abuse', where the experiences of gender and age are conflated. While literature on male rape and female rape has, in some way, universalised gendered experiences into binary categories, there is a need to recognise how a victim's emotional, physical, and psychological responses are individual and subjective. Each victim will hold a different response to their assault, and male victims suffer real trauma. Trauma is heightened by hegemonic masculinity that scaffolds how shame and stigma are experienced following sexual assault. Yet, despite the research that shows how male victims are seriously impacted mentally and physically, there are very few resources to help men heal from their assaults, The activist feminist movement of #MeToo served to raise public consciousness about sexual assault, yet it was met with mixed responses when men used it at a platform to disclose their own abuse.

#Me(n)Too?

In 2017, the hashtag phenomenon of #MeToo was highly visible and popularised on social media, particularly Twitter. The original #MeToo movement was started by African American civil rights activist Tarana Burke in 2006, who began to use the phrase 'Me Too' on social media to raise consciousness about sexual abuse and assault. In 2017, following the criminal sex acts and assaults committed by an influential film producer in the USA, the movement provided a digital platform for activism, in which many women were able to stand in solidarity, calling out experiences of sexual abuse, assault, harassment, and discrimination (Fileborn and Loney-Howes, 2019; Stiebert, 2019). Soon after, a further hashtag trend began, where '#MeToo' was relexicalised to #MenToo, by a wave described in the media as 'meninism'.[13] One of the forerunners to the popularity of #MenToo was based in India, where men's activist groups sought to raise consciousness around legislations which they perceived as anti-men. 'Meninists' in Delhi protested against the proposal of a scheme which allowed free public transport for women, in order to increase the number of women using public transport and thereby making travel safer for women. India has been reported as the most dangerous country for women, with a higher risk of sexual violence or being forced into slave labour than anywhere else globally.[14] The positive discrimination afforded to Indian women through this new initiative was, however, seen by meninists as negative discrimination against men.[15] The proposed scheme for women sought to protect against gender and sexual violence, but no such intervention, they argued, was in place for men. Nor was there protection for men against women's false allegations of rape. Despite the protests from the meninists, the proposal was subsequently accepted by the Indian government and put into place.

The purpose of #MenToo was thus bifurcated. The hashtag's popularity was used in different ways, demonstrating how it has functioned as a headline tag that allows for multiple interpretations. First, it denoted concern from the meninist movement in India about the increased support to women amid false allegations against men accused of sexual abuse; it was further used globally by men who did not want to be implicated by the phrase #MeToo, drawing responses such as 'Not All Men'. Second, #MenToo also provided men with a platform where they can share their own stories about being victims of sexual violence. The hashtag was used by men to express solidarity with women who had been abused, while other men began to share their own stories of being sexually harassed, assaulted, or raped. Many of these stories had previously been hidden because of the shame that pervades all victims of abuse, as well as the myths around male abuse that deny men can be victims.

Responses to the #MenToo movement were mixed, mainly because of the different origins and intentions of the use of the term. Valid concerns were expressed that a grassroots digital movement revived by feminist activists was being co-opted by men. Other individuals, including men themselves, ridiculed the movement, reinforcing the myth that men are only ever abusers and therefore cannot be the abused. Academics likewise weighed in on this topic. Within academic literature on #MeToo, David Purnell uses a variation on the hashtag in his article '#Me(n)Too: Storying a Male-on-Male Sexual Assault' (2019). The article is an autoethnography of Purnell's own sexual assault and he notes the importance of the feminist roots of the movement, stating that 'men will never be as systemically subjected to sexual assault as women are' (2019: 227). Detailing his own sexual abuse perpetrated by friends of his brother, Purnell describes how he was invited to a party, supposedly to celebrate the life of his brother who had recently passed away. There, he was drugged and rendered unconscious, before being surrounded by people as he lay naked and uncovered. In addressing the concern about #MeToo being re-appropriated by men, Purnell cautions: 'Share your stories, by all means, just not under the MeToo hashtag' (2019: 227). Despite this concern, he still uses the hashtag's popularity in his own article, as he offers the following comment:

> I want to point out the precariousness of not wanting to appropriate an important movement for women by using this title. I did want to borrow from the hashtag's popularity to bring attention to the importance of not silencing men who have also been sexually assaulted.
> (Purnell, 2019: 235)

Purnell's position reflects some of the concerns with men's attempt at inclusion in the movement, either through #MeToo or #MenToo, namely that some men do not wish to distract from the feminist concerns or from women who are part of the movement, but at the same time, there exists no similar popular platform for men to share their own experience of sexual violence.[16] As noted earlier, male rape is so often silenced or ignored because of stigma, shame, and hegemonic masculinity. Some of these same issues can be seen in the dynamics of men and their relationship to #MeToo. The first dynamic exposes how men are unable to share the same platform as #MeToo precisely because they are part of the problem. A second dynamic demonstrates the prevalence of one of the myths of sexual abuse: namely that men are deemed to be too strong and powerful to be abused or raped in the first place. Therefore, #MeToo does not seem to be a platform for men, irrespective of facts about sexual violence against men and men's own vulnerabilities. A third, and related, dynamic is that other men are unhappy because their hegemonic masculinity is perceived as being under threat by men who disclose their abuse and reveal their status as victims.

#ChurchToo

Alongside the scrutiny given to limited and dangerous ideals of hegemonic masculinity, the #MeToo movement has resulted in public scrutiny of institutions, and Christian communities are no exception to this. The ChurchToo hashtag[17] was adopted by survivors of sexual violence in church settings, reflecting the ubiquity of women's abuse by men, including church leaders, within these settings. The hashtag is credited to Emily Joy and Hannah Paasch, who started the #ChurchToo movement with the simple aim of sharing #MeToo stories experienced in church organisations.[18] The movement continued to make public the experiences of sexual abuse, mostly those experienced by women,[19] but also boys and men. Whereas #MeToo exposed powerful men who had assaulted women, through #ChurchToo, the silence surrounding child sexual abuse, including the victimisation and silencing of young boys by church leaders and the cover up of this abuse by church authorities, started to receive attention on mainstream social media platforms. In one example, the #ChurchToo hashtag was also used to follow the 2018 case investigated by the Supreme Court of Pennsylvania, which produced a 1,300-page report that confirmed 300 predator priests in the state had abused more than 1,000 children since 1947, a large proportion of whom were boys.

#ChurchToo became a global phenomenon,[20] and by 2017, it was reported to have reached 85 countries.[21] The hashtag is largely used by individuals and organisations with the intention of calling out abuse: sharing media reports of sexual abuse against women and children (especially boys) and documenting lawsuits against clergy. #ChurchToo operated similarly to #MenToo in offering a platform for male survivors to break the silence, have a voice, and recognise the sexual violence suffered by others. Yet, it struck out further, beginning to expose cherished notions of Christian masculinities that were harmful and needed further interrogation and dismantling. As I discuss in the following section, these harmful ideals of masculinity can be seen playing out in men's ministries within some Christian organisations, and in the Bible itself.

Hegemonic masculine ideals are rooted in and sanctioned by Christian spiritualities. In 1 Corinthians 16:13, Paul urges, 'Be watchful, stand firm in the faith, act like men, be strong', a motif often used in men's prayer groups in evangelical traditions. Joseph Gelfer (2009) proposes that masculine spirituality and masculine religious identities tend to sustain patriarchal spirituality. He notes that masculine spirituality in the evangelical men's movement is often framed through the lenses of violence and sport. Gelfer highlights how the metaphor of violence builds on the 'Pentecostal preoccupation with spiritual warfare' (2009: 61). Being a boy or man in this sense is associated with being a warrior, as the names assigned to various men's ministry groups attest: Top Gun Men's Ministries, Band of Brothers, On Target Ministries, Battle Zone Ministries, Noble Warriors, and Real Man Ministries, to cite just a few examples (Gelfer, 2009: 63–64). Gelfer also explores the connection between gym culture and sports for Christian men in his discussion of 'muscular spirituality',[22] noting how some branches of Christianity perpetuate hegemonic masculinity. He concludes by acknowledging the contribution that gay spirituality and queer theory can make for a wider view of masculinities, gay or straight. This offers a counter-narrative to toxic masculinities and patriarchal privileges in the formation of Christian masculine ideals.

Although he does not deal with rape culture or sexual abuse against men directly, Gelfer's work provides food for thought about how performative spiritual masculinities relate to and perpetuate hegemonic masculinity. Also working on men's spiritualities in church contexts, Robert Berra (2018) draws more explicit parallels with rape culture and men's ministries, arguing that certain Christian men's ministries can help to maintain rape culture through the transmission of rape myths. He notes how 'the complicity of religions with violence and patriarchal control over those who are not men (or do not meet an ideal standard of manhood) is well established' (2018: 28). Berra cites Christian teachings which validate masculine ideals, including how men render women subordinate, how sexual purity is regulated, the validation of male authority, and men's 'rightful' roles as church leaders and heads of the household.

Christian teachings on gender roles and relationships, such as those discussed by Berra (2018) and Gelfer (2009), are often substantiated through the interpretations of biblical texts. The Bible is punctuated with violent accounts which demonstrate and exemplify idealised manliness, but what about cases when men transgress such masculine ideals? Attention now turns to explore the role of religious homophobia and how this obfuscates sexual violence against men.

The role of religion in obfuscating sexual violence against men

A male victim of abuse is acutely aware of the associations between his status as both a victim and a man in a culture of toxic masculinity. Stigma and shame therefore prevent reporting in a majority of cases, and men are reluctant to seek out support. For heterosexual victims, there is a 'fear of queer' – being incorrectly assumed to be gay or bisexual because of the assault – while for men who are bisexual or gay-identifying, this leads to further questioning or rejection of their sexuality, or, through internalised homophobia, a feeling that the sexual assault was somehow merited or deserved on account of their 'deviant' sexuality. In the final section of this chapter, I examine the connections between sexual violence against men and religiously sanctioned patriarchy, misogyny, and heteronormativity. I investigate how a fear of feminisation and a fear of queer perpetuate myths around sexual violence against men. This not only is damaging for male victims but also perpetuates rape culture for women and lesbian, gay, bisexual, trans, queer/questioning, and otherwise (LGBTQ+) people.

There is a culture of stigma and shame surrounding same-sex attraction and relationships, whether through socially and culturally enforced norms or as a product of colonisation. This plays out in legal and religious spheres, from the criminalisation of 'sodomy' to contemporary conservative Christian intolerance of LGBTQ+ people. Religiously fuelled homophobia can be seen in aggressive pronouncements such as 'God Hates Fags!'

from Westboro Baptist Church, to microaggressions such as ecclesial policies that prohibit same-sex marriage in places of worship or sensationalist debates in the media intending to provoke controversy about LGBTQ+ identities being somehow irreconcilable with faith identities.

At the time of writing, the official positions from the majority of Christian churches is that homosexuality is not in line with Christianity. It is rendered a 'sin'. The Roman Catholic tradition describes homosexuality as 'a more or less strong tendency ordered toward an intrinsic moral evil and thus the inclination itself must be seen as an objective disorder'.[23] The Anglican tradition holds the line that homosexuality is 'incompatible with Scripture'[24] and that bisexual people should *choose* heterosexuality.[25] These positions are often supported by scriptural references to the destruction of Sodom and Gomorrah. Indeed, Genesis 19: 1–29 has been more popularly utilised as a clobber text to condemn homosexuality. The story relates how the townsmen of Sodom surround Lot's house and demand that the male guests who are lodging with him be brought outside so the townsmen can 'know' them, a familiar biblical euphemism for having sex. In an attempt to avoid an horrific act of male–male rape, Lot offers up his two virginal daughters in place of his honoured guests. After the townsmen refuse this offer, Lot's guests (who happen to be divine messengers sent by God) strike them blind so they cannot see their way to break into Lot's house. Lot and his family eventually escape, and God destroys the cities of Sodom and Gomorrah with fire and brimstone as punishment.

This biblical narrative is undoubtedly a text that describes attempted male rape (more on this in Chapter 2). Yet traditional interpretations of the text, and its cultural legacy, move away from highlighting the horror of sexual violence evoked therein. The term Sodom has become lexically connected to the words 'sodomy' and 'sodomite'; such is the significance of the biblical passage in creating negative, legalistic language around anal sex between men. The threatened sexual assault of men becomes conflated with homosexuality. In the process, an intended act of sexual violence has been reframed and misrepresented in order to demonise male same-sex encounters. Traditional interpretations of Genesis 19: 1–29 have focussed on the condemnation of homosexuality, and this continues to be the case across religious traditions today. In the collective religious imagination, then, *both* male rape and homosexuality are deemed sinful and punishable by God.

The perilous consequences of reading Genesis 19: 1–29 as a condemnation of homosexuality

Reading Genesis 19: 1–29 as a condemnation of homosexuality has three perilous consequences, which together are much more far-reaching than simply being a harmless biblical interpretation, a formation of theology, or an ideological position. These consequences have social and cultural import and devastating consequences for women, men, and LGBTQ+ groups. Traditional interpretations of Genesis 19: 1–29 as a text about homosexuality are damaging as they provoke (i) a perpetuation of rape culture; (ii) violence against LGBTQ+ groups; and (iii) an obfuscation of sexual violence against men.

The first consequence is that such a reading perpetuates myths that sustain rape culture. One prevailing rape myth is that rape equates to sexual desire or attraction, rather than being an exercise of power through sexual violence. The myth makes an erroneous assumption that the perpetrator relates to the victim in a manner that determines their sexuality: it therefore makes rape about sex, rather than about violent abuse. To read Sodom and Gomorrah as a text about gay sexual attraction serves to perpetuate the rape myth. Sonia Waters (2017) explores this idea, noting how homophobia is built on misogyny. She argues that Christianity's focus on same-sex relations is a deflection from the issue of sexual violence. For Waters, the text raises significant questions relating to gendered assumptions about the bodily integrity of women and LGBTQ+ people. 'Those who believe God rained down fire and brimstone at the threat of gay sex', she argues, 'seem to assume that God would have been less angry and less destructive if the Sodomites had raped Lot's daughters instead' (2017: 275). Waters rightfully continues by noting the legacy of this story in religious institutions; as she states, 'there are many people who are outraged about men having nonviolent, consensual sex with men, but violent sexual assault against women fails to produce the same level of concern' (2017: 277). I agree entirely with her argument that the rape of women has become more normative than same-sex relationships in Christian tradition:

> Rape stories in the Bible have never garnered much weight in Christian ethical teaching. Preachers do not preach on them. Christian cultures do not uphold rape as a particularly contemptible sin. Christian churches do not picket at the courthouses on rape as the cornerstone of moral abjection or societal decay as they do with same-sex relations. Congregations do not offer programs to change those whose lifestyle sexually objectifies women in the way they try to deprogram gays and lesbians.
> (Waters, 2017: 275)[26]

The second consequence of interpreting the text as a condemnation of same-sex attraction or activity is that the violence narrated in the ancient text has explicit associations and lineage with religiously fuelled homophobic, transphobic, homonegative, and transnegative attacks today. There is a common association of Genesis 19: 1–29 with religious condemnation of homosexuality and same-sex relationships. God's punishment of Sodom and Gomorrah is cited by conservative Christians as the biblical basis that provides authority to justify their prejudice against same-sex relationships. Holly Joan Toensing explains:

> Verbal expressions of this association are used against gays, lesbians, bisexuals, and transsexuals at rallies or functions. For example, one might see slogans such as 'Homosexuality = Death' (Gen. 19) or 'God Hates Fags' (Gen. 19: 24–25) written on placards held high by Christian Right groups protesting a gay and lesbian pride parade.
>
> (2005: 61)

Toensing presents a case that the sexuality of the townsmen in Genesis 19: 1–29 is likely to be heterosexual rather than homosexual. She makes visible the female characters by imagining how we might read Lot's daughters back into the text, in order to shed light on the text as non-homophobic but one in which men are engaged in battles of aggressive masculinity. For that reason, she states, 'the women of this story emerge only as possessions of heroes and husbands, as war booty, as bartering commodities in social and political deals, and as pawns in theological challenges' (2005: 74). That LGBTQ+ people are still very vulnerable to violence is demonstrated by the sheer prevalence of homophobic attacks that take place around the globe every day. And in countries where homosexuality remains illegal (punishable by corporal punishment, imprisonment, or the death penalty), homosexuality can indeed equal death.[27] Toensing draws parallels between the biblical text and its contemporary interpretations that are used to justify violence, highlighting how 'the assumption that the men of Sodom and Gomorrah were homosexually orientated likely influences individuals who act aggressively or violently toward gay men, lesbians, bisexuals, and transsexuals today' (2005: 62).

The third consequence of interpreting Genesis 19: 1–29 as a condemnation of homosexual desire, and pertinent to the thesis of this book, is that historically, religion, while bolstering hegemonic masculinity and sanctioning heteronormativity, has led to a blindness to male sexual abuse. Shame and stigma around same-sex relations is a result of religious teaching and traditional biblical interpretations of this passage. Thus, heteronormative ideals obfuscate male sexual violence and perpetuate myths around male sexual abuse. This is problematic in terms of assessing disclosures and support for men who have been victims of sexual violence, but especially for gay and bisexual men who have long been considered deviant vis-à-vis the regulation of heterosexuality, and therefore their abuse is equated with such deviancy. Simply put, there is a fear of queer, as I go on to discuss.

Misogyny and fear of queer

In ancient cultures, men and women were not seen in binary or complementary opposition; rather, as Colleen Conway puts it, a 'woman was understood not as the biologically opposite sex of man but as an imperfect, incomplete version of a man' (2003: 164–165). Daniel Boyarin (1995) argues how the practices traditionally thought of as same-sex desire, forbidden in the Torah, in the culture of the biblical and Talmudic periods, and in late antiquity, are not concerned with homosexuality, per se, but revolve instead around the issue of gender. Boyarin illustrates how the classical world was divided into penetrators (always men) and the penetrated (boys, men, and women):

> Adult free males penetrated. Some preferred boys and some women, and many liked both. There was something pathological and depraved, however, in the spectacle of an adult male allowing his body to be used as if it were the body of a person of penetrable status, whether the man did so for pleasure or for profit.
>
> (1995: 341)

In the ancient imagination, therefore, a man should not willingly assume the passive status in same-sex activity, as being penetrated by another man would equate to a loss of status, shame, and stigma. Men who were penetrated were humiliated simply because penetration was an act that a man did to a woman. Indeed, both parties in the male same-sex encounter were censored: the man who 'feminised' the other and the one who was penetrated. Stephen Greenberg illuminates how, in biblical times, the act of being penetrated equated to 'self-castration' (2004: 202). The man who is passive takes on the prejudice and discrimination which is attributed so freely to women in many cultures. Thus, for a man to be 'feminised' is the most shameful act and a total humiliation. Like Waters earlier, Greenberg also notes the connection between homophobia and misogyny in Leviticus 18: 22, where God speaks to Moses about unlawful sexual relations: 'Do not have sexual relations with a man as one does with a woman; that is detestable'. In his reading of this verse, Greenberg shows the ultimate fear is taking the position of a woman:

> Leviticus seems to claim that all intercourse between men cannot help but be a degrading, abominable humiliation of one male by another. In many ancient cultures being penetrated by another male was the height of disgrace because in being so used, one was cast into the realm of women.
>
> (2004: 192)[28]

There is therefore a toxic trio of patriarchy, misogyny, and heteronormativity at the core of hegemonic masculinity and the social and cultural scripts that remain dominant because of this triangulation. Patriarchy promotes misogyny through ingrained prejudices, discrimination, and inequalities towards women. Heteronormativity is the incessant expectation and policing of heterosexuality as the default. The fear of feminisation equates to a fear of queer. Eve Kosofsky Sedgwick uncovers how male homosocial bonds are structured through a psychologised, and I would add, pathologised, homophobia. The male homosocial spectrum, which Sedgwick describes as the 'potent and embattled locus of power over the entire range of male bonds' (1990: 9), operates in opposition against the homosexual. In terms of sexual violence against men, hegemonic masculinities rely on subordinate and subjugated forms of masculinity in order to exert their power. The binary is extraordinarily potent, despite its simplicity: it positions 'real' men against 'feminised' men.

It is not just in biblical studies where this link between misogyny and homosexuality has been drawn: the connections have also been observed in the wider academic literature surrounding male rape. Javaid notes how the feminised position has consequences on the masculine identities of those men who have been sexually abused. Thus, he states:

> male rape victims are placed at the bottom of the gender hierarchy because of their identification, emasculation and stigmatisation. Consequently, these victims are seen as challenging and contradicting the status quo, and the gender expectations and social ideals of men. Men are not expected to be victims, vulnerable, hurt, damaged, emotional and sensitive; by enacting these traits, however, they are not achieving hegemonic masculinity and are not seen as 'real' men.
> (Javaid, 2018: 200)

So far, in this chapter I have focussed on hegemonic masculinities or toxic masculinities. C. J. Pascoe and Jocelyn Hollander use the term 'hybrid masculinities' (2016: 68) to demonstrate how men are still able to reaffirm patriarchy and use their status, as dominant men, to publicly reprimand others who commit sexual violence. They discuss a football match in Oregon, USA, where the players used the feminist slogan 'No means no!' as a victory chant, aimed at shaming perpetrators of sexual violence. Yet, Pascoe and Hollander observe how this reaffirms patriarchy in new ways; as they state, 'young men can simultaneously position themselves as "good guys" who don't rape while symbolically engaging with sexual assault to signal the dominance that is constitutive of Western masculinity' (2016: 68). The sexual assault in which they engage is the emasculation of other men, who are not 'man' enough to get sex from a woman through their own sexual desirability, muscularity, or sportsman-like status and therefore 'need' to resort to rape. Through hybrid masculinities, patriarchy remains intact: women are sexualised and subservient in ways that are now hidden as acts of allegiance. Patriarchy and heteronormativity are, as ever, problematic for rape culture. Pascoe and Hollander describe this as an act of 'mobilizing rape', as 'practices, discourses, and symbols associated with sexual violence and assault may be deployed in the service of masculine dominance at interactional, discursive, structural, symbolic, and global levels' (2016: 69). Hybrid masculinities and toxic masculinity are rooted in a commitment to patriarchy and male power and dominance. They further enforce rape myths, equating rape with sexual desire and sexuality.

Hegemonic masculinity and heteronormativity function in stigmatising and shaming for all men, regardless of their sexuality. Indeed, there is an impossible irony in the machine of heteronormativity that it even damages heterosexual men who are victims of sexual violence. Yet, this dialogical relationship between heteronormativity and masculinities allows us to ascertain and assess the impact of sexual violence against gay/bisexual men and transgender persons. Those who display non-normative expressions of gender or sexuality will have already experienced the policing and challenging of their masculinity throughout their childhood, formative years, and adult lives. Rape myths that equate rape with sexual desire permit further harmful and inaccurate perceptions against male victims who identify as trans, gay, or bisexual. This is confirmed by Mitchell et al. (1999), who conducted a psychological study in which they explored attitudes to see if members of the general population attributed a degree of responsibility to victims of male rape themselves. Their study found that male rape victims were considered to be more responsible for their assault if they were gay or bisexual than if they were heterosexual. The underlying assumption that perpetuates myths around rape culture is that the victim would have experienced some pleasure from the assault because of their sexuality. This, in turn, results in a perceived reduction in the level of trauma imagined to have been experienced. Whereas male victims are blamed more than female victims (Davies et al., 2001), this is further compounded if the victim is trans, gay, or bisexual. Widespread homonegativity, homophobia, and bias against trans people and gay and bisexual men reveal how performative gender expectations and roles exist in relation to misogyny and homophobia. This, in turn, silences and stigmatises all victims of sexual assault and renders rape culture normative. Pascoe and Hollander (2016) examine how this process has spread into popular culture, noting that satirical cartoons about politicians may use an image of a man being penetrated to attack the virtues of the subject's masculinity. They give the example of Saddam Hussein, noting how figurative rape is an expression of 'power over' another, wherein one's gender and sexual identity can be dominated and humiliated. Inviting reflection on this, Pascoe and Hollander state:

> Consider, for example, the wartime cartoons . . . that depict multiple variations of Saddam Hussein being anally penetrated by a SCUD missile, which symbolically represented American military might at the time. These cartoons positioned a (male) America as militarily and culturally dominant through symbolizing male–male rape.
>
> (2016: 75)

Sexual violence is one of the most ancient weapons of war, as it traditionally demonstrates dominance of the perpetrator and disgrace to the victim and this is seen in the biblical texts themselves (see Chapter 2). In this sense, rape is not simply a by-product of the war itself; it is intrinsic to the military assertion of dominance (Buss, 2009). Male rape in wartime also reveals how rape myths about sexual violence against men are accepted among victims, demonstrating how cultural and social factors impact the survivor's perceptions of their assault, leading to feeling of shame, guilt, and self-blame (Voller et al., 2015). The shame and stigma of male rape, therefore, make it such an effective weapon of war.

Conclusion

Explorations of men and masculinity have formed part of the critical debates in studies of sexual violence. Outside of biblical studies, research into male rape, especially in the disciplines of sociology and psychology, has sought to answer urgent questions and investigate the shame and stigma around male rape by exposing the myths that surround this form of gendered violence. With its interdisciplinary focus, this chapter has examined the impact of abuse and rape against men, while articulating the surrounding shame and stigma in light of the zeitgeist of #MeToo. Critical readings of contemporary masculinities demonstrate a lineage of patriarchy and heteronormativity that actively discriminate against women, LGBTQ+ people, and, ultimately, male victims of sexual violence. Hegemonic masculinity and heteronormativity obfuscate sexual violence against men, and, as I have noted, religion plays a determining role in this machinery, through misogyny and fear of queer. In Chapter 2, I offer further discussion of religion's role in silencing male rape through my explorations of the scriptures in the Hebrew Bible, noting how contemporary attitudes towards sexual violence against men draw parallels in the Bible itself.

Notes

1 '1 in 6'. Available: https://1in6.org/. The statistic is based on research conducted in the USA.
2 In the UK, male rape was only designated as an offence in 1994. In a media report the following year, Commander Tom Williamson, Metropolitan Police, stated: 'Male rape is clearly one of the easiest crimes to get away with in this country at the moment. The likelihood of being convicted is remote in the extreme' (cited in Hodge and Canter, 1998: 222).
3 UK Law Sexual Offences Act, 'Rape', 2003. Available: www.legislation.gov.uk/ukpga/2003/42/section/1.
4 UK Law Sexual Offences Act, 'Causing a Person to Engage in Sexual Activity Without Consent', 2003. Available: www.legislation.gov.uk/ukpga/2003/42/section/4.
5 The legal definition of rape involving a penis is equally problematic where women perpetrate unwanted penetration on other women.
6 There is significant under-reporting of sexual violence against women, and therefore published data and statistics are not fully representative nor do they provide an accurate picture of the total number of abuse cases. The World Health Organisation notes how men are even less likely than women to report being a victim of sexual violence: Available: www.who.int/violence_injury_prevention/resources/publications/en/guidelines_chap2.pdf.
7 Office for National Statistics, 'Sexual Offences, Appendix Tables', 08 February 2018. Available: www.ons.gov.uk/peoplepopulationandcommunity/crimeandjustice/datasets/sexualoffencesappendixtables.
8 Estimated numbers relating to these percentages are as follows: sexual assaults on men 631, compared with women 3,371; rape on men 54, compared with women 1,068; indecent exposure or unwanted touching on men 606, compared with women 3,189. A recent case of unwanted touching became public during the Six Nations rugby match, in which Alun Wyn Jones' genitalia was grabbed by Joe Marler during the game. Marler faced a ten-week ban as a consequence of his actions, yet many commentators, including legal ones, declared the action to be not sexual assault. Several reports even described the action as 'fondling', unable to render a man a victim of sexual assault. Defence of Marler focussed on the definition of 'sexual' and its association with desire, not sexual assault, in which the perpetrator's unwanted touching led to humiliation on behalf of the victim. Unwanted touching is clearly an act of powerful assertion and sexual violence and should be labelled as such. The frequency of such acts in sport and in locker room culture means that it is an act of sexual violence that is not named and is hidden in plain sight. Sexual violence becomes normalised under the heading of 'having a laugh' or 'banter', which renders the victim as humourless should they call out their abuse.
9 National Sexual Violence Resource Center, 'Statistics About Sexual Violence', 2015. Available: www.nsvrc.org/sites/default/files/publications_nsvrc_factsheet_media-packet_statistics-about-sexual-violence_0.pdf.
10 According to the NSVRC, 40.2% of gay men and 47.4% bisexual men compared with 20.8% heterosexual men reported sexual violence other than rape during their lifetimes.
11 See also Turchik and Edwards, 2012.
12 Overall, rates of suicide for men are at their highest. In the UK, the Samaritans Suicide Statistics Report states that men are more than three times more likely

to die by suicide than women, the highest rate being among men in the 45–49 age group. Scotland has seen the highest rate of suicide in young men, between the ages of 15 and 24, an increase of 52.7%. Reponses to such rates can be seen in the activities of charity organisations set up specifically to promote projects aimed at encouraging men to talk, including CALM (Campaign Against Living Miserably) in the UK and Male Suicide Prevention Australia. The Suicide Prevention Resource Center in the USA is engaged with projects specifically aimed at preventing suicide in men, given the accessibility of firearms to men in the USA as one of the major causes of suicide death. Similar to the statistics in the UK, men whose age range falls into the 'middle years' are more at risk. The World Health Organisation produced a comprehensive set of data pertaining to rates with intersectional data such as age, gender, and income. Available: www.who.int/mental_health/prevention/suicide/suicideprevent/en/.

13 Hannah J. Davies, 'Meninism, #MeToo and Murder: Clique, Teen TV's Most Political Show, Returns', *The Guardian*, 06 November 2018. Available: www.theguardian.com/tv-and-radio/tvandradioblog/2018/nov/06/meninism-metoo-and-clique-teen-tvs-most-political-show-returns.

14 Belinda Goldsmith and Meka Beresford, 'India Most Dangerous Country for Women with Sexual Violence Rife – Global Poll', *Reuters*, 26 June 2018. Available: https://in.reuters.com/article/women-dangerous-poll/india-most-dangerous-country-for-women-with-sexual-violence-rife-global-poll-idINKBN1JM076.

15 Pallavi Pundir, '#MeToo has Shaken up Men's Rights Activism in India, and the Result is #MenToo', *Vice*, 06 June 2019. Available: www.vice.com/en_in/article/8xzd3g/metoo-has-shhaken-up-mens-rights-activism-in-india-result-is-mentoo.

16 See Bianca Fileborn and Rachel Loney-Howes (eds.). *#MeToo and the Politics of Social Change* (Palgrave MacMillan, Cham, 2019) for detailed discussion on the exclusionary effects of #MeToo as a white, heteronormative, and US-centred campaign, including chapters on the exclusion of Aboriginal women or LGBTQ+ people.

17 Originally #ChurchToo was used largely by those who experienced abuse in evangelical Christianity. It pushed against harmful church teaching that encouraged silence and submission of women. Female survivors of this abuse described how such teachings were grounded in biblical 'authority', such as Ephesians 5: 22: 'Wives, submit yourselves to your own husbands, as you do to the Lord'. Many women who had endured sexual abuse within evangelicalism used the self-definition of 'ex-vangelical' on social media, adapting the term to show how they had left evangelicalism. The phrase from Ephesians 5: 22 feeds into biblically sanctioned hegemonic masculine ideals: the notion of men being dominant and powerful.

18 Hannah Paasch, 'Sexual Abuse Happens in #ChurchToo – We're Living Proof and Purity Culture Teaches Women That It's All Their Fault', *HuffPost*, 04 December 2017. Available: www.huffingtonpost.co.uk/entry/sexual-abuse-churchtoo_us_5a205b30e4b03350e0b53131?ri18n=true&guccounter=2.

19 The impact of uncovering sexual abuse occurring in church settings through #ChurchToo was immediate. In one instance, Bill Hybels, the senior pastor at Willow Creek Community Church in Chicago, resigned alongside his board of senior elders amid allegations of misconduct and cover-ups of sexual abuse. Hybels was publicly accused by multiple women of sexual misconduct. For details, see Bob Smietana, 'Bill Hybels Accused of Sexual Misconduct by Former Willow Creek Leaders', *Christianity Today*, 22 March 2018. Available: www.christianitytoday.

com/news/2018/march/bill-hybels-misconduct-willow-creek-john-nancy-ortberg. html. A further example in 2018 was Pastor Andy Savage from Highpoint Church in Memphis, who confessed to the sexual assault of a girl in 1998 when he was working as a youth pastor. The victim, Jules Woolson, described how Savage had groped her breasts and forced her to perform oral sex on him. After his confession and admission, Savage was initially applauded by his congregation because he asked for their forgiveness, yet he omitted telling them certain details and described the event as a 'sexual incident' rather than an assault. For details, see Kate Shellnutt, '#ChurchToo: Andy Savage Resigns from Megachurch over Past Abuse', 20 March 2018. Available: www.christianitytoday.com/news/2018/march/andy-savage-resigns-abuse-megachurch-standing-ovation.html.

20 Whereas #MeToo was considered US based, white, and heteronormative, #ChurchToo was global from its inception, recognising the proliferation of sexual abuse by clergy across the globe. It also looked at harmful traditional teachings from churches against LGBTQ+ people.

21 Casey Quackenbush, 'The Religious Community Is Speaking Out Against Sexual Violence With #ChurchToo', *Time,* 22 November 2017. Available: https:// time.com/5034546/me-too-church-too-sexual-abuse/.

22 In mobilising examples from popular culture, Katie Edwards highlights that the images of Jesus used in advertising represent a 'Sporting Messiah', infused as they are with ideologies of militarism, nationalism, and war. She states how 'Christ-imagery is used as a vehicle through which brands can construct and communicate values about masculinity, male sexuality and patriotism, and the adverts present the sports stars as gods among men, messiahs come to redeem their nations' (2012: 342). Elsewhere, Deryn Guest reflects on the illustrative representations of men in the *Children's Bible in Colour,* noting how they epitomise physical attributes associated with attractive masculinity: 'Gideon, with his designer stubble, strong chin, head scarf manfully arranged, sending his soldiers forth into battle. The scantily clad, muscle-honed, luxuriantly haired Samson battling with lions . . . Jehu: another muscularly defined Adonis, appealingly adorned in a bright blue loincloth' (2016: 46).

23 Congregation for the Doctrine of the Faith (1986), 'Letter to the Bishops of the Catholic Church on the Pastoral Care of Homosexual Persons'. Available: www. vatican.va/roman_curia/congregations/cfaith/documents/rc_con_cfaith_doc_ 19861001_homosexual-persons_en.html.

24 Anglican Communion Office (1998 Lambeth Conference, published 2005), 'Lambeth Conference Resolutions Archive Index of Resolutions from 1998'. Available: www.anglicancommunion.org/media/76650/1998.pdf.

25 The House of Bishops state 'if God's overall intention for human activity is that it should take place in the context of marriage with someone of the opposite sex, then clearly the Church needs to encourage bisexual people who are capable of entering into such a relationship to do so' (House of Bishops, 2003: 283).

26 Waters also notes the parallels between Genesis 19: 1–29 and Judges 19, noting how the former is more widely known than the latter: 'The story of the concubine and her horrific rape (Judges 19) has virtually no symbolic place in popular Christian imagination. It is possible to spend many years of Sundays in church without hearing the story of Judges 19–21. While "Sodomite" has become a catchphrase in modern culture for men who engage in sexual relations with men, there is no word in Western culture that references the gang rape of a woman in Judges 19. There is no term "Gibeahite" that plays its part in the

lexicon of straight sexual relations to evoke disgust or fear, condemnation or prohibition. There is no flurry of Judges quotations from popular preachers in prophetic response to court cases that have freed rapists' (2017: 281).

27 The data set for December 2019 from ILGA World – the International Lesbian, Gay, Bisexual, Trans and Intersex Association – notes how it is illegal to be LGBT in 70 states around the world. The death penalty is in effect in six countries, and possible in another six; in 26 countries, same-sex relations are punishable by more than ten years to life imprisonment, and a further 30 countries have up to eight years of imprisonment. Available: https://ilga.org/maps-sexual-orientation-laws.

28 Greenberg also notes how traditional Jewish daily prayers involve a man praising God for not making them a gentile, a slave, or a woman (2004: 197). The lines are found in the preliminary morning prayers known as *birkhot ha-shahar* or the 'dawn blessings'. The alternative prayer said by women is 'Who has made me according to His will'.

References

Abdullah-Khan, Noreen. 2008. *Male Rape: The Emergence of a Social and Legal Issue*. Hampshire: Palgrave Macmillan.

Berra, Robert. 2018. 'Men's Ministries and Patriarchy: From Sites of Perpetuation to Sites of Resistance'. In *Rape Culture, Gender Violence and Religion: Christian Perspectives*. Edited by Caroline Blyth, Emily Colgan and Katie B. Edwards. Cham: Palgrave Macmillan, pp. 27–52.

Boyarin, Daniel. 1995. 'Are There Any Jews in "The History of Sexuality"?' *Journal of the History of Sexuality*, 5/3: 333–355.

Buss, Doris E. 2009. 'Rethinking "Rape as a Weapon of War"'. *Feminist Legal Studies*, 17/2: 145–163.

Connell, Raewyn W. 1995. *Masculinities*. Cambridge: Polity Press.

Conway, Colleen M. 2003. '"Behold the Man!" Masculine Christology and the Fourth Gospel'. In *New Testament Masculinities*. Edited by Stephen D. Moore and Janie Capel Anderson. Atlanta: Society of Biblical Literature, pp. 163–180.

Coxell, Adrian W. and Michael B. King. 2010. 'Male Victims of Rape and Sexual Abuse'. *Sexual and Relationship Therapy*, 254: 380–391. Reprinted from *Sexual and Marital Therapy*, 113/1996: 297–308.

Davies, Michelle, Paul Pollard and John Archer. 2001. 'The Influence of Victim Gender and Sexuality on Judgments of the Victim in a Depicted Stranger Rape'. *Violence and Victims*, 16: 607–619.

Edwards, Katie B. 2012. 'Sporting Messiah: Hypermasculinity and Nationhood in Male-targeted Sports Imagery'. In *Biblical Reception*. Edited by J. Cheryl Exum and David Clines. Sheffield: Phoenix Press, pp. 323–346.

Eigenberg, Helen. 1989. 'Male Rape: An Empirical Examination of Correctional Officers' Attitudes Toward Rape in Prison'. *The Prison Journal*, 692: 39–56.

Exum, J. Cheryl. 2016 [1993]. *Fragmented Women: Feminist Subversions of Biblical Narratives*. Second Edition. London: Bloomsbury.

Fileborn, Bianca and Rachel Loney-Howes (eds.). 2019. *#MeToo and the Politics of Social Change*. London: Palgrave Macmillan.

Gelfer, Joseph. 2009. *Numen, Old Men. Contemporary Masculine Spiritualities and the Problem of Patriarchy*. London: Equinox.

Graham, Ruth. 2006. 'Male Rape And The Careful Construction Of The Male Victim'. *Social & Legal Studies*, 15/2: 187–208.

Greenberg, Stephen. 2004. *Wrestling with God and Men: Homosexuality in the Jewish Tradition*. Wisconsin: The University of Wisconsin Press.

Greene, Mark. 2018. *The Little #MeToo Book For Men*. New York: ThinkPlay Partners.

Groth, A. Nicholas and Ann W. Burgess. 1980. 'Male Rape: Offenders and Victims'. *American Journal of Psychiatry*, 137: 806–810.

Guest, Deryn. 2016. 'Modelling the Transgender Gaze'. In *Transgender, Intersex, and Biblical Interpretation*. Edited by Teresa J. Hornsby and Deryn Guest. Atlanta: SBL Press, pp. 45–80.

Harding, James E. 2018. 'Homophobia and Rape Culture in the Narratives of Early Israel'. In *Rape Culture, Gender Violence, and Religion: Biblical Perspectives*. Edited by Caroline Blyth, Emily Colgan and Katie B. Edwards. Cham: Palgrave Macmillan, pp. 159–178.

Hawkins, Lindsey G., Natira Mullet, Cameron C. Brown, Dane Eggleston and Julie Gardenhire. 2019. 'All Survivors Have the Right to Heal: A #Metoomen Content Analysis'. *Journal of Feminist Family Therapy*, 31/2–3: 78–99.

Hodge, Samantha and David Canter. 1998. 'Victims and Perpetrators of Male Sexual Assault'. *Journal of Interpersonal Violence*, 13: 222–239.

hooks, b. 2000. *Feminism is for Everybody: Passionate Politics*. London: Pluto Press.

House of Bishops. 2003. *Some Issues in Human Sexuality: A Guide to the Debate*. London: Church House Publishing.

Javaid, Aliraza. 2016. 'Feminism, Masculinity and Male Rape: Bringing Male Rape "Out of the Closet"'. *Journal of Gender Studies*, 25/3: 283–293.

Javaid, Aliraza. 2017. 'In the Shadows: Making Sense of Gay Male Rape Victims' Silence, Suffering, and Invisibility'. *International Journal of Sexual Health*, 294: 279–291.

Javaid, Aliraza. 2018. 'Male Rape, Masculinities, and Sexualities'. *International Journal of Law, Crime and Justice*, 52: 199–210.

Javaid, Aliraza. 2019. 'What Support? Foucault, Power, and the Construction of Rape'. *Qualitative Sociology Review*, 151: 36–60.

Knowles, Gordon J. 1999. 'Male Prison Rape: A Search for Causation and Prevention'. *The Howard Journal of Criminal Justice*, 38: 267–282.

Mitchell, Damon, Richard Hirschman and Gordon C. Nagayama Hall. 1999. 'Attributions of Victim Responsibility, Pleasure, and Trauma in Male Rape'. *Journal of Sex Research*, 36/4: 369–373.

Pascoe, C.J. and Jocelyn A. Hollander. 2016. 'Good Guys Don't Rape: Gender, Domination, And Mobilizing Rape'. *Gender & Society*, 30/1: 67–79.

Purnell, David. 2019. '#MenToo: Storying a Male-on-Male Sexual Assault'. *Journal of Loss and Trauma*, 243: 226–237.

Scholz, Susanne. 2010. *Sacred Witness: Rape in the Hebrew Bible*. Minneapolis: Fortress Press.

Sedgwick, Eve Kosofsky. 1990. *Epistemology of the Closet*. Berkeley: University of California Press.

Sivakumaran, Sandesh. 2005. 'Male/Male Rape and the "Taint" of Homosexuality'. *Human Rights Quarterly*, 27/4: 1274–1306.

Stiebert, Johanna. 2019. *Rape Myths, the Bible and #MeToo*. London: Routledge.

Toensing, Holly Joan. 2005. 'Women of Sodom and Gomorrah: Collateral Damage in the War against Homosexuality?' *Journal of Feminist Studies in Religion*, 21/2: 61–74.

Trible, Phyllis. 1984. *Texts of Terror: Literary-Feminist Readings of Biblical Narratives*. Philadelphia: Fortress Press.

Turchik, Jessica A. and Katie M. Edwards. 2012. 'Myths About Male Rape: A Literature Review'. *Psychology of Men & Masculinity*, 13/2: 211–226.

Voller, Emily, Melissa A. Polusny, Siamak Noorbaloochi, Amy Street, Joseph Grill and Maureen Murdoch. 2015. 'Self-Efficacy, Male Rape Myth Acceptance, and Devaluation of Emotions in Sexual Trauma Sequelae'. *Psychological Services*, 12/4: 420–427.

Waters, Sonia E. 2017. 'Reading Sodom through Sexual Violence Against Women'. *Interpretation: A Journal of Bible and Theology*, 7/3: 274–283.

Weiss, Karen G. 2010. 'Too Ashamed to Report: Deconstructing the Shame of Sexual Victimization'. *Feminist Criminology*, 53: 286–310.

2 Sexual violence against men in the Hebrew Bible

Introduction

Male rape myths are at play in biblical texts, which serve as sources of authority in religious communities. Moreover, biblical texts are culturally and socially significant; historically, they have been used for law-making and for swearing oaths in court. Culturally, the Bible has been powerful in shaping works of literature, art, music, and film. As the Bible sustains patriarchy and hegemonic masculinity, it is undoubtedly problematic for rape culture. In this chapter, I note its impact on sexual violence against men specifically. Hegemonic masculinity is interwoven within the fabrics of societies and cultures, so ideals of being a 'real' man are biblically and religiously sanctioned. Tackling rape culture has become prominent through social and cultural enlightenment about the issue of sexual violence afforded by the #MeToo, #MenToo, #ChurchToo, #JesusToo, and other social media activist projects. Yet, germane to my argument is that myths perpetuating sexual violence against men not only are a contemporary issue, but are also actually found in the biblical texts. Sexual violence is as old as the ancient texts themselves, and that includes sexual violence against men. Accounts of rape are narrated in the Hebrew Bible, and through contemporary eyes, these reflect attitudes of misogyny and homophobia that serve to protect patriarchal, hegemonic masculinity.

Chapter 1 has explored the myths, stigma, and shame that surround sexual violence against men in society, culture, and religious institutions. This chapter examines the concept of masculinity in the Bible in order to contextualise the content of the biblical texts I go on to examine. My discussion of male sexual violence in the Hebrew Bible is then set out in two parts. There are no explicit cases of actual male rape through anal penetration, but there are examples of forced penetration, men receiving unwanted sexual advances, and men evading rape and women being offered up as victims in their stead. In my exploration of the biblical texts, I first deal with actual sexual assault against men, offering three passages as lenses: Lot and his daughters (Genesis 19: 30–38), Joseph and Potiphar's wife (Genesis 39), and the attempted rape of men (Genesis 19: 1–29; Judges 19). The case of forced penetration is the most obvious example of sexual violence against a man, as Lot's daughters get their father drunk in order to have sex with him (Genesis 19: 30–38). Potiphar's wife, a woman without a name of her own in the text, makes unwanted sexual advances against Joseph, and she makes a false sexual assault allegation against him.[1] One of the insights about sexual violence against men is that shame and stigma are often conceptualised as less of a problem for women than for men (Javaid, 2019). This proves to be the case biblically speaking, as demonstrated in Genesis 19: 1–29 and Judges 19, where women are offered as replacement victims for the men, who are the original intended victims, as though the rape of a woman is somehow less shameful than the rape of a man. The second part of the chapter is concerned with the metaphorical enactment of sexual violence against men, and here I examine the texts as they are chronologically presented in the Bible: I explore Noah's nudity and the curse of Ham (Genesis 9: 20–27), Ehud's left-handed penetration of the fat king Eglon (Judges 3: 12–30), Sisera's 'penetration' at the hands of Jael (Judges 4), and also Delilah's humiliation and sexual use of Samson (Judges 16). Before concluding, I offer some further examples of biblical texts that allude to male rape.

Hegemonic masculinity in the Bible

In Chapter 1, I argued how religion, with its legacy of patriarchy, heteronormativity, and misogyny has served to fuel impossible expectations of masculinities for men. To counter concerns that a discussion of sexual violence against men in the Bible is anachronistic, in this section I focus on how hegemonic masculinity is at play in the biblical texts themselves. Before going on to discuss specific examples of sexual violence against men in the Hebrew Bible, in this short section I discuss masculinity and men across both testaments; this background is important, given the focus on Jesus in Chapter 3.

David Clines' 2015 lecture entitled 'The Scandal of a Male Bible' forms part of his influential work on biblical masculinities. He observes how 'the Bible is a male book, written by men, for men' (2015: 1). Clines uncovers how masculine performativity is constantly at play throughout biblical texts, where male values are upheld and any deviation from these social scripts has negative consequences for the men involved. Clines proposes that the male values bolstered by biblical texts include strength, violence and killing, physical size, honour, holiness, womanlessness, totality thinking, and binary thinking (2015: 2).[2]

Clines' examination of these male values remain standards and ideals by which hegemonic masculinity operates today. He mobilises examples of the representations of Jesus in the gospels to illustrate two of these values: violence and womanlessness. First, he observes verbal violence from Jesus in Luke 14: 26, 'No one can be my disciple if he does not hate his father and mother and wife and children and brothers and sisters – and his own life!' Jesus is also physically violent in the turning of the tables at the Temple described in Matthew 21: 12–13 and Mark 11: 15–18. Clines' examples of Jesus' violence in language and action is largely approved of by biblical scholars, as it aligns with modern notions of masculinity; as he argues, 'all biblical scholars, mind you, approve entirely of Jesus' violence, and never see a trace of rampant masculinity here' (2015: 4).

Hegemonic masculinity reinforces man's dominant position through the subordination of women and other marginalised masculinities, such as gay men and trans people. The subordination of women is explicit in Clines' argument, as he observes their insignificance and disposability in the biblical texts. With regard to the second male value of womanlessness, Clines finds examples in the characterisations of Jesus, David, Paul, and Yahweh. He explains the apparent disposal and casualisation of relationships with women as presented through David:

> It is a striking feature of the David story that the males are so casual about women, and that women are so marginal to the lives of the protagonists. There is in this story, on the whole, no sexual desire, no love stories, no romances, no wooing, no daring deeds for the sake of a beloved. This is not a world in which men long for women. It is rather a matter of pride for David and his men, in fact, that they have kept themselves from women.
>
> (Clines, 2015: 9)

Clines offers examples in Jesus' ministry of his support and positive relationships with a number of women but observes that, like David, Jesus does not need women. It is important to highlight, though, that Jesus' needlessness is still less reprehensible than the treatment of women by other men in the Bible. Clines comments ironically, 'Jesus is such a womanless man, and he shows it first and foremost by not being married. No matter his reasons. It is actually a very ostentatious way of signalling, Women? Who needs them?' (2015: 10). I return to focus specifically on Jesus and his sexuality and purity in Chapter 3.

When men are not womanless, they have significant duties to uphold the honour and purity of the women for whom they are responsible. Indeed, each time a woman is raped within the biblical traditions, a man, usually her father or husband, is also deemed to be violated, as it is a man who holds the rights to the woman's body and sexuality. The cultural code of not being man enough to protect one's property or to be duped and killed by a woman all speaks back to contemporary cultures of hegemonic and toxic masculinity. In 1 Samuel 31, we learn that Saul is critically wounded (v.3) and he begs his armour-bearer, 'Draw your sword and run me through, or these uncircumcised fellows will come and run me through and abuse me'. His armour-bearer refuses through fear, so Saul takes his own sword and falls on it (v.4). The armour-bearer does the same (v.5). The next day, the Philistines come to strip the dead; they cut off Saul's head and strip off his armour (v.9). The stripping and enforced nudity of one's enemies are usually trophy-acts following victory in war. In a similar suicide because of fear of his emasculation, Abimelek asks his armour-bearer to kill him when he is mortally wounded by a millstone dropped on his head by an unnamed woman, so as to avoid being remembered as someone killed by a woman (Judges 9: 54).

Of course, women as well as men experience shame and stigma through involuntary nudity. Indeed, so significant is the association between nudity and shame that it shapes the opening book of the Hebrew Bible from the outset, in the story of Adam and Eve. We see that in Genesis 2: 25, 'The two of them were naked, the man and his wife, yet they felt no shame'. By Genesis 3: 7 the feelings are reversed, as Adam and Eve realise their nakedness and look for fig leaves to cover themselves: 'Then the eyes of both of them were opened, and they realized they were naked; so they sewed fig leaves together and made coverings for themselves'. By Genesis 3: 10, the feeling of shame is fully realised and unequivocally connected to nudity, as Adam says to God, 'I was afraid because I was naked; so I hid'.[3]

In contrast to the shame and vulnerability encoded by involuntary nudity, voluntary nudity is a potential symbol of male aggression and always representative of power dynamics. There are examples where the penis itself actually represents hegemonic masculinity and power relations between men. There is the correlation between testimony and testicle, in which oaths are thought to be sworn on male genitalia. In Genesis 24: 2–9, Abraham's servant swears an oath to find a wife for Isaac by placing his hand under the thigh of his master. A similar interaction with male genitalia occurs in Genesis 47: 29, where Joseph is required to put his hand under his father's thigh to make the promise to bury him in Canaan, not Egypt. In these texts, such interactions showcase assertions about masculinity, as this ritual act serves to demonstrate the status and authority of a man; both actions to patriarchal figures are gestures of submission and obedience to authority. A more frivolous encounter with patriarchal penises occurs in the exhibitionism of David dancing wearing only a linen ephod (2 Samuel 6: 14). Here, male nudity is sexualised and boastful, aware though as David and Michal are that this sort of nudity is still undesirable as a form of self-abasement. In response to Michal's fury, David recognises how his own actions are deemed shameful: 'I will become even more undignified than this, and I will be humiliated in my own eyes. But by these slave girls you spoke of, I will be held in honour' (2 Samuel 6: 22). Another boastful example of male nudity is found in 1 Kings 12: 10. Rehoboam seeks the advice from the elders who had served his father and makes a direct correlation between his penis size and masculine prowess: 'my little finger is thicker than my father's loins'. The sexual imagery is striking; Ken Stone describes it as 'a striking instance of sexual rhetoric that plays upon the symbolic association between male genital size and the dynamics of dominance and submission' (2006: 230).

In other places in the Hebrew Bible, we have further examples of male nudity and exposure. In the introduction to the prophet in Isaiah 20, the Lord says how Isaiah walked naked and barefoot for three years (v.2). So significant is Isaiah's nudity that the description is repeated in the following verse (v.3). Verse 4 reinforces this nudity one final time with emphasis on the 'buttocks bared'. Isaiah's compliance to God's demand to walk unclothed and without shoes still carries a sense of involuntary nudity, hence Isaiah's shame, rather than a ritualised display of his masculine phallic prowess, as noted in the examples earlier. Rhiannon Graybill comments that 'the prophet's nakedness is humiliating, even shocking; it is also necessary to the work of the prophecy' (2016: 2), and she notes how male nudity is disturbing in the biblical traditions. Graybill uncovers two further consequences of this that go unaddressed by the narrator: the first is Isaiah's pain walking for three years barefoot; second, and most significant for my argument here, is that the nudity is shaming:

> Isaiah's nakedness has specific consequences for his experiences of masculinity and embodiment. What Isaiah does with his body troubles expectations of what a male body ought to do, and how it ought to appear. Visual and textual evidence from the ancient Near East shows that male nakedness and vulnerability are linked, for example, to the humiliation of prisoners of war. Such humiliation also activates gender categories and understandings of gender performances: humiliating a man is frequently linked to stripping away his culturally recognized masculinity.
>
> (Graybill, 2016: 3)

Thus, while voluntary male nudity is connected to pride and boastful expressions of dominance, horror is expressed at involuntary male nudity, which is considered a source of great shame. Another example of enforced nudity is found in Genesis 37: 23, where Joseph is stripped of his ornate robe and thereby rendered vulnerable. The stripping of men and women always serves to humiliate, and in warfare often seems to be a prelude to rape (Lamentations 1: 8–10; 3), including the 30 unnamed Philistine men who are killed and stripped in Judges 14: 19. Also, in 1 Samuel 18, David goes out and kills 200 Philistine men and returns with their foreskins in exchange for permission to marry Saul's daughter, Michal. Traditional readings of this text have not shone a light on the men who were genitally violated by David and his troops, whether before or after their murder. Elsewhere, in 2 Samuel 10, King Hanun is persuaded that David's envoys have come under the pretence to offer David's sympathies but are really there to spy and seize the kingdom (v.3). David's envoys are shamed and rendered vulnerable, as 'Hanun seized David's envoys, shaved off half of each man's beard, cut off their garments at the buttocks, and sent them away' (v.4).

Thus, whether voluntary or involuntary, nudity is tied up with sociopolitical structures, hierarchies, status, and theological interpretations. But forced male nudity in the Hebrew imagination is almost always negatively connected to loss of status or humiliation. Traditional expectations of biblical men are the same as those represented and maintained today through hegemonic masculinity. In turn, hegemonic masculinity obfuscates sexual violence against men. There are numerous further examples of men being assaulted – physically, metaphorically, and socially – in the Hebrew biblical traditions, as I examine in the following section.

Sexual violence against men

Lot and his daughters (Genesis 19: 30–38)

After their escape from Sodom, Lot lived in a cave with his two daughters in the mountains. In their isolation, the eldest daughter was concerned about being unable to have children, as there were no men about. She concocts a plan with her younger sister to get their father drunk on wine and then to sleep with him in order to get pregnant to preserve the family line. Once he is drunk, the eldest daughter has sex with Lot while he is unaware of what is happening (v.33). The next night, the scenario is repeated with the younger daughter, and again, Lot is oblivious to what is going on (v.35). The plan is a 'success', in that both daughters are impregnated as they desired. The older daughter has a son, Moab (who becomes ancestor of the Moabites) and the younger daughter also has a son called Ben-Ammi (who becomes ancestor of the Ammonites).

Lot's daughters perpetrate sexual assault against their father, once they have inebriated him with alcohol. This counters the myth that girls or women are not perpetrators of sexual violence, and that men cannot be victims. The text also speaks to contemporary rape culture in which alcohol is associated with sexual assault in a high number of cases, where it is used in order to disinhibit or incapacitate a victim. Abbey et al. (2004) state that over half of all sexual assaults are linked to alcohol use, by the perpetrator or the victim, or both.[4] Rape culture is also ubiquitous in media articles which suggest that the victim is somehow to blame if they have left themselves vulnerable to being raped due to their alcohol consumption, reinforcing erroneous stereotypes about victims who drink. Such myths perpetuate rape culture by shifting responsibility away from the perpetrator to the victim.

A number of crimes, transgressions, and taboos take place in the story of Lot and his daughters: forced penetration of the father, incest, and inbreeding. The deception of the daughters dishonours the father. Here we have a scene where the women are perpetrators, but note how their actions are fuelled by desire for procreation, considered a noble aim in the biblical texts, rather than a sexual motive. Progeny is paramount. Moreover, their sexual assault is almost celebrated through the generative achievement of their plan and the birth of their sons. Martin Kessler and Karel Deurloo describe the event as one of 'emergency incest' (2004: 120). Benno Jacob goes as far as stating that the daughters' actions are heroic, as he states:

> [the daughters] do not act out of lust but in order to fulfil their womanly destiny and preserve their lineage. Given this highest purpose for them as women, all their misgivings recede. For this purpose, they give themselves over as sacrifices and their action derives from the utmost heroism.
> (1934: 464–465; translated and cited in Stiebert, 2013: 134)

The reader is left wondering about the impressive fertility awareness of the daughters and at what point Lot asked his daughters who fathered their children.

Lot's unconsciousness through drink renders him entirely inactive; there is no lengthy description of him taking the passive sexual role usually reserved for women or any acknowledgement that an assault has occurred. Indeed, Esther Fuchs (2003) observes the neutrality of the narrator's voice in relating the crimes that take place in the story. Lot's dignity remains intact despite his passivity. There is no condemnation from him, and no immediate response to his daughters' actions. A number of commentators suggest that this scene is a countermove to the father's offer of the daughters to the Sodomites in Genesis 19: 8, discussed further below (see Scholz, 2010). In terms of consequences, Teresa Hornsby points to the legacy of the Moabites and the Ammonites as foreigners and enemies of the Israelites further on in the text and describes them as 'incestuous bastards' (2007: 154, cf. Bailey, 1995: 132).

Yet Lot is not entirely blameless or exonerated in the view of some interpreters. Elke Seifert (1994; cited in Stiebert, 2013) views the story as one in which a male sexual fantasy is able to play out, including a father's incestuous, and therefore transgressive, desire for his daughters. The absence of Lot's wife is also noticeable, as she became a pillar of salt in the previous story after transgressing the angelic commandment not to look back at the burning cities of Sodom and Gomorrah (Genesis 19: 1–29). Seifert reverses the role of the characters in the story, making Lot the perpetrator and his daughters the victims. Seifert's reading relies on contextual material not located in the text itself, as she suggests that the text should be read from the perspective of the girls who are incestuously violated, and that the narrative is constructed in a way to protect the father. I urge an exercise of caution with this approach. What we have here is a narrator, and subsequent interpreters, who share a reluctance in naming the event by what is described: an act of sexual assault against a man. Being unable to name it as sexual abuse further perpetuates the myths around sexual violence against men discussed in Chapter 1: namely, that men cannot be sexually abused, and that girls and women cannot be perpetrators of sexual violence. Moreover, Lot's story speaks back to the myth around male rape that the presence of an erection or ejaculation implies consent. Lot is narrated as being unaware of both of his assaults, and therefore unable to consent.

The story of Lot and his daughters concludes at the end of Genesis 19, and chapter 20 then returns to the story of Abraham. Lot is left with no victim status, or even an explicit self-awareness that he has been raped. The narrator allows the text to pass without any real examination of the horror of what has happened; there is no time or space afforded to reflect on the nature of the sexual assault and the crimes perpetrated against him. The actual case of male sexual assault is shrouded in silence, indicative of contemporary attitudes and experiences of men who have been abused.

Joseph and Potiphar's wife (Genesis 39)

Whereas female beauty can lead to sexual vulnerability in the Hebrew Bible, as in the case of David and Bathsheba (2 Samuel 11), male beauty can also lead to exposure to sexual harm. In Genesis 39, we are told that Potiphar, an Egyptian who is one of Pharaoh's officials, is master to Joseph. The narrator emphasises three times how Joseph is put in charge of the household (vv.4, 5, and 6). Joseph is described as 'well-built and handsome' (v.6), and his master's wife asks him to come to bed with her. Joseph resists Potiphar's wife, noting that to have sex with his master's wife would be to wrong his master and God (v.9). While Joseph resists, Potiphar's wife persists: 'she spoke to Joseph day after day, he refused to go to bed with her or even be with her' (v.10). In verse 11, she makes a pass at Joseph, again asking him to go to bed with her, while taking hold of his cloak. When Joseph makes his escape, she is left holding the cloak in her hand. In verse 14, Potiphar's wife falsely accuses Joseph of rape. When Potiphar learns of this, he is enraged and sends Joseph to prison.

Potiphar's wife breaks biblical gender expectations, and in her pursuit of Joseph takes the active role usually reserved for men, such as we see in the story of David and Bathsheba. The woman is the perpetrator of the unwanted sexual attention; the man is the victim. Susanne Scholz notes how there is a twist to the telling of this story in the Qur'an (Sura 12), which describes Joseph's beauty as divine and angelic, and therefore impossible to resist. A longing for Joseph in this way could reflect a longing for God:

> Ms. Potiphar's women neighbors gossip about her attraction to a slave; in turn, she invites them to her house so that they may see for themselves the attractiveness of 'Yusuf'. She gives them fruit knives when Joseph enters the room. Because the women cannot take their eyes off him, they end up cutting themselves into their fingers and exclaim: 'Glory be to God, this is not a human being; this is an honorable angel' (Sura 12:31).
> (Scholz, 2010: 165)

Joseph's reserve and the mastery of his own sexual urges clearly demonstrates the virtues of self-restraint and abstinent sexuality. This restraint is clearly valued by the Lord, who shows his favour as a reward. Both biblical and cultural receptions of this text often position Joseph as commended for his sexual virtue and control, rather than portraying him as a victim of sexual assault and false rape allegations (Levinson, 1997). The story is therefore interpreted as one that depicts the importance of chastity, focussing on Joseph's virtue rather than the crime of Potiphar's wife.

Indeed, the nature of abuse against Joseph is two-fold: the persistence of Potiphar's wife in lavishing unwanted sexual attention on him and her subsequent false allegation of attempted assault when her advances are rebuffed. The unwanted sexual attention is further exacerbated by the power dynamics between the two, as Joseph is Potiphar's slave and would thus be considered the property of the household, without any recourse to consent or to withhold consent to any sexual act perpetrated against him. The gendered expectations are reversed in this scene, and this unexpected reversal only reaffirms the stereotype that women should not demonstrate sexual agency. The scene narrates a controlling woman claiming to be vulnerable against the advances of a man, even though Joseph is the one who actually holds no power.

Hegemonic masculinity is seen to have weak foundations, as Joseph's intersecting identities of slave and Hebrew all render him vulnerable to abuse, regardless of his masculinity. Indeed, his powerlessness makes the accusation against him more ironic. Not only does Genesis 39 demonstrate distinct abuses of power, but the scene is also overlain with racist assumptions about the sexual dangers posed by foreign men, as Potiphar's wife refers to Joseph as 'the Hebrew'. Joseph is thus sexually and culturally 'othered'.

Joseph's status as slave and property of the household draws parallels with Abram and Sarai's sexual exploitation of Hagar (Genesis 16), as Michael Carden notes:

> Joseph can be seen as representing the plight of household servants or domestics who are subjected to harassment and abuse, sexual and otherwise, by their employers. Furthermore, in the ancient world the master of the house had the right of sexual access to all his slaves, male and female.
> (2006: 56)

In a similar vein, Ron Pirson (2004) speculates on the reasons for why Joseph was brought into the household, including the possibility of Joseph's function in Potiphar's plans for the Hebrew slave to father a child with his wife:

> It was Potiphar's idea to bring Joseph to them, so that he could sleep with his master's wife, and therefore, considering Potiphar's physical condition, to father a child with her. So, this might support the idea that Joseph has a role comparable to Hagar.
> (2004: 236)

Pirson continues, 'This is why Potiphar cannot keep Joseph in his household any longer: the attractive and good-looking youth (39, 6) did not do the thing he was intended to do, . . . here is the reason Potiphar burns with anger' (2004: 259).

Readers tend to sympathise with Joseph, contrasting his treatment with abusive episodes experienced more often by women. Scholz agrees, noting, 'interpreters take Joseph's side unhesitatingly. They read *with* the androcentric narrative' (Scholz, 2010: 166). Potiphar's wife becomes an image of the archetypal woman scorned and a 'manifestation of the feminine frightening to men' (Niditch, 2012: 44). In discussing the sexual assertiveness of biblical women, Johanna Stiebert notes that Potiphar's wife is not the only sexually forward woman. Following Brenner (1985), Stiebert suggests that female sexual forwardness is often considered by interpreters as acceptable if the intention is to procreate and produce an heir, and she draws parallels with

Lot's daughters' violation of their father. What is not surprising from this argument, as we saw with Lot and his daughters, is that unwanted advances and sexual assault for procreative reasons allow for the sexually abusive episodes to be explained away, sympathetically interpreted or justified. Stiebert avoids this, however, as she affirms:

> There is no dispute that Potiphar's wife's behaviour is appalling: she is a privileged woman, the wife of a powerful man, who abuses her power over Joseph, a Hebrew slave, by commanding and pestering him for sex, seizing (or perhaps, groping) him and then accusing *him* of attempted rape and sending him to prison.
>
> (2019b: 107)

Stiebert's discussion makes an important point about the unfounded myth of false rape allegations articulated in the story of Potiphar's wife and Joseph: namely, that women often accuse men of rape because they were rejected or regret a sexual encounter. While false rape allegations cause considerable harm and damage to men, it is a dangerous misconception that such allegations are brought with considerable frequency. Their rarity attests to how legal proceedings and media sources perpetuate rape culture by raising similar questions to victims.[5]

What happened to Potiphar's wife? Similar to Lot's daughters, there is no immediate consequence to her actions: no punishment, whether familial, legal, or divine. Joseph is not the only victim of her crime, but her betrayal to her husband is also a side product of this transgression that passes without explicit mention.

One of the other myths surrounding male rape is that a man is 'lucky' to receive even unwanted sexual attention from women, and if he does not respond to this, then his heterosexuality and masculinity are questionable. Sexual experiences with girls and women, especially older women, serve to bolster a man's status as a 'real' man. Joseph's rejection of Potiphar's wife's advances, and his subsequent punishment due to her false allegation, serve as an example of an abusive, coercive, and exploitative sexual experience. As discussed in the previous chapter, contemporary understandings of an abusive episode such as this can lead to a diminished capacity for trust, intimacy, and further emotional and psychological disturbances. Indeed, these could be further impacted through his unjust imprisonment, as in Joseph's case.

The attempted gang rape of men (Genesis 19: 1–29; Judges 19)

Genesis 19: 1–29 narrates the story of Sodom and Gomorrah and, as discussed in Chapter 1 of this book, has been more broadly connected to a

Sexual violence against men in the Bible   45

disavowal of homosexuality through patriarchal and heteronormative lenses, rather than an actual examination and naming of the attempted rape of men. Two angels arrive in Sodom and Lot meets them, convinces them to stay with him and eat with him (vv.1–3). Before they go to bed, all the men from the city, of all ages, come to Lot's house and surround it (v.4). They call to Lot, 'Where are the men who came to you tonight? Bring them out to us so that we can have sex with them' (v.5). Lot goes outside to speak with the men, and shutting the door behind him, he pleads with them, 'Don't do this wicked thing' (vv.6–7). He offers up his two virgin daughters instead: 'Let me bring them out to you, and you can do what you like with them. But don't do anything to these men, for they have come under the protection of my roof' (v.8). The men persist at the door (v.9), but the two angelic men reach out and pull Lot back into the house, shutting the door (v.10). Lot's guests blind the men who are outside so that they can no longer find the door (v.11) and tell Lot to get everyone out of his house as they are about to destroy the place (vv.12–15). The angelic men take the hands of Lot's wife and his daughters to lead them out of the city and they tell Lot to flee to the mountains (vv.16–17). Lot asks the men to allow him to go to a nearby town, and they grant the request saying they will not overthrow this town (vv.18–23). The Lord rains down burning sulphur on Sodom and Gomorrah and the entire cities and inhabitants are destroyed (vv.24–25). Lot's wife, however, breaches the instruction not to look back; she looks back at the burning cities and becomes a pillar of salt (v.26). The next morning, Abraham is witness to the destruction and the smoking remains of Sodom and Gomorrah (vv.27–28).

This narrative depicts unequivocally an attempted male-on-male gang rape. Lot goes to extreme lengths to prevent this from happening, even offering the would-be rapists his two virginal daughters instead. The hospitality shown to relative strangers is sharply contrasted to the treatment of the women, his daughters, who are offered as substitutes without their consent.

Judges 19 tells a very similar story of attempted male-on-male rape, in which a woman is brought in as a bargaining tool in exchange for the protection of a man. In the opening of Judges 19, a Levite goes travelling to collect his wife who had run away to her father's home in Judah (possibly because she has been unfaithful to him; vv.1–2). The Levite stays with his father-in-law for three days, and on the fourth day, he leaves with his wife to go back home (vv.4–10). On the return journey, they stop at Gibeah to spend the night. There, they are offered shelter by an elderly man who meets them in the town square (vv.11–21). The story then takes a shocking twist, showing the efforts of a host to protect his Levite guest from being gang raped by the wicked men of Gibeah, who shout to the old homeowner, 'Bring out the man who came to your house so we can have sex with him' (v.22). The homeowner pleads,

> No, my friends, don't be so vile. Since this man is my guest, don't do this outrageous thing. Look, here is my virgin daughter, and his concubine. I will bring them out to you now, and you can use them and do to them whatever you wish. But as for this man, don't do such an outrageous thing.
>
> (v.23)

When the men of Gibeah initially refuse this offer, the Levite seizes his wife and pushes her out the door to the waiting crowd. The townsmen take her, then rape and abuse her throughout the night (v.25). At dawn, she returns to the house where her master is staying, falling at the doorway (v.26). The man tells her to get up, but there is no answer. He puts her on his donkey and sets off for home (v.27). What follows is shocking and horrific, as the Levite takes a knife and cuts up his wife, limb by limb, into 12 parts, and sends them to all areas of Israel (v.29), in order to provoke civil unrest and war (see Judges 20). The text is ambiguous as to whether or not she is dead before this act of butchery.

The responses from Lot and the host in Gibeah are almost identical – do whatever you want with these girls, but 'don't do this wicked thing' (Genesis, 19: 6) and 'don't do such an outrageous thing' (Judges 19: 24) to a man. Both of these narratives are testimony to how men were honoured and revered in Israelite cultures, and sexual abuse against women was deemed less harrowing than sexual abuse against men. Moreover, male rape was seen as shameful, as it demoted the penetrated victim to the position of a woman, as noted in Chapter 1.

In her interpretation of this text, J. Cheryl Exum (2016 [1993]) notes the concubine's previous sexual betrayal, suggesting that her sexual autonomy is threatening to patriarchal ideology and serves as a major source of male anxiety. Thus, according to Exum, 'the symbolic significance of dismembering the woman's body lies in its intent to de-sexualize her' (2016 [1993]: 144). Exum's analysis of Judges 19 also highlights significant points from the text in relation to male rape culture. In dispelling the myth that acts of male rape are connected to homosexuality, she asks:

> Does this mean that all these men of Gibeah are homosexuals? Hardly. Rape is a crime of violence not of passion; homosexual rape forces the male victim into a passive role, into the woman's position. The men of Gibeah want to humiliate the Levite in the most degrading way.
>
> (Exum, 2016 [1993]: 145)

Sexual violence against men in the Bible 47

The text thus subverts one of the myths of male sexual abuse that connects male victims and perpetrators to homosexuality. Exum describes the substitution of the men for the woman as 'androcentric ideology', noting how 'homosexual rape is too threatening to narrate' (2016 [1993]: 146). Likewise, in the case of Lot's rapes at the hands of his daughters, male rape is unimaginable and therefore impossible to describe by the narrator. Significantly, even though the level of violence throughout the Hebrew Bible is high (Clines, 2018), to narrate male rape would be a step too far. While the exchange of victim is part of an economy of hospitality (Stone, 1996; Reaves, 2016), the apparent interchangeability of victim (from men to women) in both scenes is indicative of the underlying cultural attitudes of rape and sexual violence: rape is more about power and control than sexual desire. Michael Carden articulates how

> male rape in Genesis 19 and Judges 19 is an act of homophobic violence signifying the abuse of outsiders and the breach of the community of Israel. Male rape serves to reinforce the heterosexuality of the insiders by inscribing outsiders as queer and queers as outsiders.
>
> (1999a: 47)

James Harding takes this idea further, noting how the text 'is part of the genesis of the symbolic violence of Jewish and Christian homophobia' (2018: 159). As I observed in Chapter 1, traditional heteronormative interpretations muddy the readings of these texts in Jewish and Christian traditions, such that the suggestions of violent male rape are conflated with any consensual same-sex act, as biblical readings bolster arguments against homosexuality in religious and public spheres.

Metaphorical enactments of sexual violence against men

Noah, Ham, and the curse of Caanan (Genesis 9: 20–27)

In Genesis 9: 20–27, Noah gets drunk from the fruits of his vineyard and lays uncovered inside his tent (v.21). In comes his youngest son, Ham, who sees his father naked and tells his two brothers outside (v.22). His brothers, Shem and Japheth, take a garment to cover their father's nudity, and walk in backwards with their faces turned so they do not actually see his naked body (v.23). Noah awakes from his drunken stupor and takes offence at what his son Ham has done to him (v.24); he immediately curses Caanan, Ham's son, making him the lowest of slaves, while Shem and Japheth are praised (vv.25–27). It is interesting to note how it is Ham's son who is cursed and not Ham himself.

John Bergsma and Scott Hahn note how wine is a symbol of sexuality and the vineyard is 'a place of lovemaking' (2005: 30). Observing a correlation between wine and sexuality in biblical and ancient literature, they make a thematic link to the account of Lot's sexual assault by his daughters:

> The similarities between the two pericopes are numerous: in the aftermath of a calamitous divine judgment, instigated by the wickedness of men – particularly sexual wickedness (cf. Gen 6: 4; 19: 5), which destroys the earth or a large part of it – an aged patriarch gets drunk, facilitating intercourse between parent and child, giving rise to one or more of the traditional enemies of Israel (Canaan, Moab, and Ammon). The parallels hardly seem coincidental.
>
> (Bergsma and Hahn, 2005: 31)[6]

It is not entirely clear what happened in the tent, but Noah's forceful reaction attests to the severity of Ham's wrongdoing. Bergsma and Hahn (2005) offer three possible reasons for the events that provoke Noah's outrage: 'Exegetes since antiquity have identified Ham's deed as either voyeurism, castration, or paternal incest. This last explanation seems to be enjoying a revival of popularity in some recent scholarship' (2005: 26). Whatever the nature of Ham's wrongdoing, the transgressions of voyeurism, castration, and paternal incest all contravene expectations of hegemonic masculinities. Bergsma and Hahn argue that if Ham's offense was, indeed, voyeurism, that would not explain the gravity of Noah's curse on Caanan. Howard Eilberg-Schwartz recalls the world within the biblical texts, noting that 'in Israelite imagination, the father's nakedness was connected with shame when the father was a passive object of someone's gaze' (1994: 87). Yet, similar to my discussion earlier in this chapter, Eilberg-Schwartz makes a distinction between voluntary nudity and involuntary nudity: 'a father was not dishonoured if he intentionally exposed his nakedness. It was his prerogative to do so' (1994: 87). Having his nakedness witnessed without his consent, Noah becomes the object of the gaze, and is thereby 'feminised' and rendered vulnerable.

There is an emphasis on Noah's response in the narrative: 'When Noah awoke from his wine and found out what his youngest son had done to him, he said, "Cursed be Canaan!, The lowest of slaves will he be to his brothers"' (vv.24–25). The phrase 'had *done* to him' suggests something more active than a voyeuristic violation. A popular rabbinic view is that Ham castrated Noah in an attempt to assume his father's authority.[7] While this provides a plausible reason for Noah's severe castigation, Bergsma and Hahn observe that 'what is lacking, however, is any lexical hint in the text of Gen 9: 20–27 that would suggest castration' (2005: 28).

Did Ham sexually abuse Noah? Gerhard von Rad suggests that 'possibly the narrator suppressed something even more repulsive than mere looking' (1972: 24). There are further clues to this in the Hebrew itself; the phrase used to describe 'to see the nakedness of the father' is similar to the phrase 'to uncover nakedness' in Leviticus 18: 7, which itself appears to be an idiom for 'sexual intercourse' (Bergsma and Hahn, 2005). Indeed, Anthony Phillips (1980) examines the Levitical expression of 'uncovering the nakedness' (18: 7) in relation to incest and sexual activity with family members. He considers the Genesis 9 text as one in which Noah was sexually abused by Ham, justifying this conclusion by focussing on the severity of Noah's reaction and punishment. The crime is parental incest and sexual assault on a drunken father. Phillips suggests that 'we should perhaps understand this incident as more than an immodest looking at his drunken and naked father but rather as his actual seduction while unconscious – an act so abhorrent that the author is unwilling to spell it out' (1980: 41). Although representations of this assault can be read as incestuous and homosexual, Ham's violation of Noah ultimately represents a hunger for power, as Ham proceeds to boast to his brothers about what he has done. To reiterate a fact that speaks back to myths around male rape: sexual assault against men is about power, rather than sexual desire.

Ehud and Eglon (Judges 3: 12–30)

The story of Ehud and Eglon begins with the Israelites doing evil in the eyes of the Lord, and the Lord gives Eglon, king of Moab, power over Israel (v.12), where he ruled for 18 years (v.14). The Israelites cried to the Lord, who sent them a deliverer, 'a left-handed man' named Ehud (v.15). Ehud made a double-edged sword that he straps to his right thigh under his clothes (v.16). When he encounters the king, we learn Eglon is 'a very fat man' (v.17). Ehud tells the king he has a secret message for him, and the king asks the attendants to leave them alone (v.19). Once alone, Ehud reaches for the sword with his left hand, draws it from his right thigh and plunges it into the king's belly (v.21). The king is so fat, that 'even the handle sank in after the blade, and his bowels discharged. Ehud did not pull the sword out, and the fat closed in over it' (v.22). Ehud locks the doors to the room, and the servants begin to wonder if the king is relieving himself (v.24), but after waiting 'to the point of embarrassment' (v.25), they unlock the doors. They see their king dead, and Ehud had gotten away.

Scholz asks, 'Where is the male-on-male rape in this narrative?' (2010: 160). She turns to Deryn Guest's analysis of the text, where Guest highlights several elements of the story that turn the scene into one in which Eglon is metaphorically raped: Ehud's left-handedness, the repetition of 'hand' as euphemism for a penis, Eglon's fatness and its association with femininity, and his Benjamite affiliation. Regarding his Benjamite status, Guest recalls how Jonathan, the young prince devoted to David 'in the Hebrew Bible's major homoerotic relationship' (2006: 172), is a Benjamite. Guest suggests the following:

> it is plausible that the author of Judges had this in mind ... we seem to have a satirical jibe at the Benjamites that gives double pleasure to the assumed Judaean reader who can laugh not only at the Moabites but also their tribal brothers who gave their loyalties to the wrong king and whose sexuality is questioned.
>
> (2006: 172)

Guest (2006) builds on the work of Stone (1996) and Carden (1999b) to highlight how 'the cultural codes of honour and shame prevalent in the ancient world have demonstrated how male rape was used as a means of dishonouring one's male rival' (2006: 182). Guest explores the text in Judges 3 as one that is suggestive of rape perpetrated by Ehud on Eglon. Eglon is rendered feminine by the description of him from his size, as Guest comments:

> Eglon is clearly being staged as one obliged to perform the traditional woman's part in a sexual encounter, that is as the one who is penetrated and passive. His fatness is thus not mentioned solely to signify greed or gullibility but to indicate his role in a male rape scene.
>
> (2006: 172)

The emphasis on Ehud's left-handedness, where the Hebrew word for 'hand' is often used euphemistically to denote genitalia, also suggests sexual deviance on the part of Ehud. As the narrator allows the reader to enjoy a tale that pokes fun at the Moabites and the text serves as a joke, Guest asserts that this is no joke for those on the receiving end of the phallic aggression. The text is saturated in toxic assumptions about masculinity; as Guest notes,

> this text assumes that to be caricatured as a passive recipient of anal rape is one of the most derogatory insults that one can direct towards a person/group. It assumes that people like Eglon *deserve* to be violated/ eliminated from society.
>
> (2006: 176; Guest's emphasis)

The text denotes the consequences for those who transgress expectations of masculinity: they become the object of jokes and ridicule, and any violation of their body is merited because of their offence against hegemonic masculinity.

Jael and Sisera (Judges 4)

In Judges 4, the prophet Deborah foretells how Sisera will not be honoured in battle and the Lord will deliver him into the hands of a woman (v.9). Following the loss of his troops, Sisera is able to flee on foot, arriving at the tent of Jael. Jael meets him, invites him in, addresses him as 'lord', and tells him not to be afraid. He enters the tent, asks for a drink of water, and she gives him some milk and covers him (vv.18–19). Sisera asks Jael to be on guard, requesting she does not disclose he is in her tent should anyone come by and ask (v.20). As Sisera lays asleep, Jael picks up a tent peg and hammer and quietly goes over to him, then drives the peg through his head into the ground and he dies (v.21).

Jael subverts gender expectations and displays both female and male virtues. In terms of gender, there is a role reversal that is quite obvious to the reader, as Judges 4 present both Deborah and Jael as women who act independently of men and in almost instinctive ways with one another, even though they never actually meet. Jael operates in biblically stereotypical male ways, through her strength, violence, and cold-blooded killing. At the same time, however, Danna Nolan Fewell and David Gunn comment that 'while Jael is neither, literally, mother nor lover to Sisera, this scene is filled with maternal and sexual imagery' (1990: 392).

Jael's sexual crimes against Sisera are two-fold: grooming and penetration. The first crime draws on the maternal symbolism in the text, while the second draws on the sexual imagery. His desperate vulnerability leads to risk and he is killed in a violent attack after his murderer claims to offer shelter and rest. Jael quickly builds a relationship of trust in order to abuse Sisera. The tactic of paying attention, reassuringly flattering him with the title 'lord', and offering a drink and rest is symbolic of the grooming stage of sexual violence and coercion.[8] If Jael is positioned as a mother figure through maternal imagery, then Sisera is child-like and therefore groomed. The situation is one in which Sisera becomes dependent on Jael, as his alternative is to return to the helplessness of the losing battle. Jael plays on his feelings of fear, distress, and confusion, and she has power and control over him. Similar to the child or young person who is unlikely to know that they have been groomed, these relationship power dynamics are hidden by the narrator in the brief episode offered. In labelling Jael's abuse as grooming, I heed Carden's warning against 'the use of terms that are loaded with stigma, in a Western context, to describe non-stigmatised behaviour in a non-Western context' (1999b: 92). While grooming is a contemporaneous term, Jael's actions are synonymous with grooming in that she offers care while plotting harm. The stigma associated with the behaviour, especially perpetrated by a woman against a man, is manifested in the biblical text through symbolism and imagery.

Moreover, Mieke Bal's description of Jael's penetration of Sisera's temple sees the act as one of sexual violence; as she states, 'the head of the hero has its vulnerable point, designated either as the neck, where the head can be severed, or as the temple, where it can be pierced, as in a reversed rape' (1992: 134).[9] Similarly, Gale Yee interprets the story of one as reversed rape: 'The author describes the killing scene as the reversal of rape (4:21). The man becomes the woman; the rapist becomes the victim; the penetrator becomes the penetrated. The tent peg in Jael's hands becomes synecdochically the ravaging phallus' (1993: 116). Sisera is thus emasculated through his grooming and physical assault at the hands of a woman, as Fewell and Gunn observe:

> Sisera's order to the woman, 'Stand at the opening . . . and if anyone comes and asks you, "Is there a man here?" say, No'. For Sisera, the answer 'No, there is no man here' is intended to be a lie, but for the reader attentive to irony, the answer 'no' reflects the truth. The mighty man has become a vulnerable child; the virile man lies impotent.
>
> (1990: 393)

The brutality of Jael's grooming, penetration, and killing is contrasted against the maternal imagery: a subtle yet powerful reminder of the traditional expectations of the representation of women in the Bible. Indeed, there are a number of maternal metaphors in the scene, noting Jael's offer of milk when Sisera requested water, covering him with a blanket as a mother would her child, and Deborah's retelling of the story in her song of praise (Judges 5: 24–27), where she describes Sisera falling between Jael's feet, symbolic of birth. Fewell and Gunn also observe how the woman's tent symbolises a woman's body, as men only really enter women's tents for the purposes of sex. The text thus challenges myths around sexual violence against men by presenting the woman as perpetrator and the victim as a man. Jael's calculated control and exerted power through her grooming and penetration of Sisera demonstrate the problematics of male abuse being silenced in the text and even celebrated by Deborah in Judges 5.

Samson and Delilah (Judges 16)

Samson was the last of the leaders who 'judged' Israel in the book of Judges (chapters 13–16). In Judges 13, Samson's mother is described as infertile and childless, and an angel of the Lord appears to her to announce that she will become pregnant and give birth to a son. The son will take the lead in delivering Israel from the Philistines (vv.1–5). The angel tells his mother than her son's head 'is never to be touched by a razor because the boy is to be a Nazirite, dedicated to God from the womb' (v.5). In Judges 16, Samson falls in love with Delilah and the rulers of the Philistines ask her to lure him and find out the secret of his great strength so that they are able to overpower him; in return, she is to be rewarded with silver (vv.4–5). Delilah wastes no time, and in the following verse she asks him directly, 'Tell me the secret of your great strength and how you can be tied up and subdued' (v.6). Samson gives her several wrong answers at first (vv.7–14), then finally, after her pressing and cajoling him, he finally tells her the truth. In verse 16, we see how she nags and prods him day after day to tell her the source of his strength, 'until he was sick to death of it'. Samson confides that a razor has never been used in his head, and if his head were shaved, his strength would leave him (v.17). Delilah puts Samson to sleep on her lap, and calls for someone to shave off the seven braids of hair on his head. This works, and his strength leaves him (v.19) and the Lord leaves him (v.20).

Why, why, why, Delilah? Scholz draws attention to the Hebrew verb *'innâ* in verses 5, 6 and 19 of Judges 16, which is often translated as 'afflict, 'weaken', 'make helpless', or 'subdue'. Yet the same verb may also be translated as 'rape' when it denotes a violent sexual act.[10] In Judges 16: 19, the use of this same verb could suggest that Delilah may have sexually assaulted Samson when he is powerless: 'After putting him to sleep on her lap, she called for someone to shave off the seven braids of his hair, and so began to *'innâ* him. And his strength left him'. Scholz comments about the use of this verb in Judges 16 and makes an astute observation that most interpreters do not comment on the verb 'because they believe it is impossible for a woman to rape a man or because they assert that this verb does not always signify rape. Yet the interpretative possibility exists' (2010: 174). Discussing the use of the verb elsewhere in the Hebrew Bible, Sandie Gravett states:

> while ancient readers possessed familiarity with the colloquial expressions that made the actions clear, modern readers simply lack the cultural contexts to accomplish such connections and to understand these texts as about rape unless the translator renders them as such.
>
> (2004: 293)

Judges 16 certainly narrates the humiliation and sexual use of Samson, as well as his symbolic castration due to the loss of his hair. Susan Niditch highlights the connection between hair and sexuality, as she asserts, 'the shearing of Samson's hair is a sexual stripping and subjugation' (1990: 616). Niditch continues:

> The defeated warrior has been made into a woman; the cutting of Samson's hair, ironically accomplished by a woman's treachery, makes him into a woman, the subdued one, the defeated warrior. In the Samson tale, the hair-cutting as symbolic castration or womanization clusters with several other images of his defeated status.
>
> (1990: 617)

Indeed, Niditch also offers further metaphorical terms used later in Judges 16 that point to sexual violence. In verse 21, the Philistines seize Samson, gouge out his eyes, and take him down to Gaza. They bind him with bronze shackles and set him to grinding grain in the prison. The grinding itself demonstrates the taming of Samson, as he engages with work usually undertaken by women or beasts. Niditch also notes that the 'grinding' image itself is used to represent 'intercourse' in other texts (Job 31: 10 and Isaiah 41: 2). Moreover, in verse 25, Samson is used 'to entertain' or 'to make sport of' and 'to perform' for the Philistines, phrases that may themselves hint at some form of sexual abuse.

Further exploring the metaphor of castration in Judges 16, Marco Derks notes that the potency and power attributed to Samson's hair has phallic connotations:

> He had made his hairstyle a symbol of what made him so unique: his masculine power. Put differently, it had become a phallic symbol. Instead of regarding his long hair as a sign of his Nazirite status, Samson took it as a sign of his gendered and sexual superiority.
>
> (2015: 569)

With a focus on symbolic sexual violence, I concur with Derks' observation that Samson's situation involved needing to prove his masculinity without making a direct reference to the biological marker of his manhood; as he notes,

> the reason for this cultural 'prohibition' – or at least reticence – to mention the penis is that it needs to be kept concealed that a penis is not always erect – that is, male strength and superiority are not a 'natural given'.
>
> (2015: 570)[11]

Gravett also sees Samson's assault as an image of castration: 'by permitting Delilah access to his secrets and his body, he takes the subordinated and victimized positions, at least temporarily, of a raped woman' (2004: 295).

Contemporary critical examinations of this text have linked the role Samson plays in his own downfall with BDSM (bondage, discipline, dominance and submission, sadomasochism). Lori Rowlett positions Delilah as the dominatrix and Samson as the submissive partner. She explores the pattern of domination and links it to a BDSM role-play scenario, commenting how 'Delilah does not trick him into saying or doing anything. Samson deliberately relinquishes control to the dominatrix who repeatedly subjects him to humiliation and bondage' (2001: 106). Therefore, parallels can be drawn in the teasing and dicing-with-death scenario. Nonetheless, Caroline Blyth (2017) warns that we should be cautious about using contemporary terms and definitions to discuss sexuality and gender relations, insightfully pointing out how any assumption of heterosexuality is equally anachronistic, too.[12] In this sense, while I applaud Rowlett's interpretation for its queer lens, playfulness, and parody, I find her argument less convincing. In my own examination of BDSM from a Christian perspective, I note how 'there is a holy trinity of BDSM, which includes mutuality, consensuality and pleasure' (Greenough, 2018: 139), and I fail to see the mutuality of the exchange, as Delilah seems enervated rather than enjoying her role if positioned as dominatrix. There is no consent given in the scene, and there is no expression of pleasure.

My discussion here points to how hegemonic masculinity depicted through the presentation of Samson is ruptured in Judges 16. The sexual imagery highlights how Samson is symbolically castrated and therefore feminised. Although following instructions from the Philistines, Delilah is integral to his abuse, that is, both physical and sexual. Niditch concludes how 'the language and imagery here partake of the epic language of the defeated warrior as a sexually subdued woman in order to emphasize the Israelite Samson's subdued and oppressed status' (1990: 617). The text speaks back to myths about male sexual violence: women can be and are perpetrators; and men can be and are victims of sexual violence. Ultimately, Samson is feminised and rendered powerless because of Delilah's intent and actions.

Further examples

Two further examples in the Hebrew Bible that allude to male rape are offered by Gravett (2004) from the books of Job and Jeremiah. She notes the use of the Hebrew verb *'innâ* in Job 30: 11 and translates the Hebrew as follows: 'for his cord he loosened and *raped* me, and restraint before me they threw off' (2004: 287; my emphasis). Gravett states:

> Once God figuratively disrobes, the description of the assault includes men coming through a wide breach (v.14), terrorizing Job, taking away

his honor and pouring out his soul (vv.15–16), and inflicting a pain that never ends (vv.17–19). The entirety of this text corresponds with the idea of a rape and the humiliation inflicted is fleshed out in the most striking fashion.

(2004: 288)

Gravett also notes how enforced nudity and sexual violence is indicated in Jeremiah 13: 22, in which the Lord tells him he has been mistreated and his skirts have been torn because of his sins. In 20: 7, Jeremiah further describes how he is overpowered by the Lord. Gravett points to another verbal root (*pth*), which carries a sense of 'to seduce, entice', but which may also carry connotations of malignant sexual attention and therefore be translated as 'to rape' (or, I might suggest, 'to groom'). She builds on the work of James Crenshaw to elaborate further:

> Jeremiah accuses God of rape. This is no trivial accusation, nor is it uttered in a flippant manner. The words are carefully chosen to cover the act of seduction and accompanying violence. . . . Jeremiah feels entirely vulnerable to the smooth words of the Lord, just as an innocent young girl is no match for experienced lovers.
> (Crenshaw, 1984: 39; cited in Gravett, 2004: 294)

The shock of such an interpretive accusation against God can provoke outraged responses. Yet, given the association of men with violence, it is unsurprising to read figurative or physical descriptions of men being 'raped'. The violence depicted in the Hebrew Bible through warfare, exploitation and sexual violence towards women should make us unsurprised to encounter the shame and stigma inflicted on some men in order to allow other men to assert their power. All of these acts of violence serve to affirm the potency of hegemonic masculinity and remind us that emasculation and dishonour form part of the economy of the social structures evoked within these ancient texts.

Conclusion

This chapter has documented how myths around sexual violence against men are at play in biblical texts, yet over two millennia later, we still have lessons to learn. The Hebrew Bible depicts both actual and metaphorical sexual assaults against men, yet these are often erased in the interpretive traditions surrounding these texts. Clearly there needs to be changes in how we interpret biblical texts, particularly in how we attribute and sanction power and control to men and both objectify *and* idealise masculinities. These are

Sexual violence against men in the Bible 57

not abstract concepts unrelated to sexual violence against men today, as they remain deeply interwoven into many religions, societies, and cultures. Through a critical examination of the biblical texts, this chapter has highlighted how men are also victims of patriarchy through the perpetuation and policing of hegemonic masculinity. Uncovering the sexual violence against men in the Bible is thus a step towards shifting cultural attitudes to male rape and sexual abuse. While I have drawn on examples of sexual violence against men depicted in the Hebrew Bible, in the following chapter, attention turns to Jesus' experience of sexual violence in the New Testament. There, I detail the problems and tensions associated with recognising the gospel accounts of Jesus' passion and own sexual abuse, while considering the role of masculinity, purity codes, and power.

Notes

1 Stiebert comments how Potiphar's wife's 'namelessness already may convey some measure of disdain – although it is not uncommon for women of the Hebrew Bible (whether named or unnamed) to be identified in relation to male relatives' (2019b: 77).
2 For 'totality thinking', Clines states how women in ancient times were focussed on the here and now, busy living their lives in the context of their homes, and they did not travel. Clines comments how men, on the other hand, are represented in times and contexts beyond their own. He offers examples in men's use of phrases, for example, 'for ever' (283 times in the Bible), 'everlasting' (61 times), 'eternal' (68 times in the New Testament)' (2015: 11). For 'binary thinking', Clines uses the idea of men categorising groups into 'us' and 'them', such as allies and enemies.
3 In Hebrew contexts, Michael Satlow argues that nudity is an offence against God (1997: 431). In rabbinic interpretations, male nakedness involves uncovering what is holy; as Satlow explains, 'for the rabbis, male nakedness means exposure of the penis. The rabbis understand exposure of the penis in the sancta as an offense against God' (1997: 431). Similar to Clines' discussion in this section, Satlow notes that the rabbinic literature is androcentric, and therefore any concern with female nudity only relates to the reaction that it draws from men. One of the specific concerns is that female nudity may result in sexual arousal and sexual misconduct in men. This is exemplified particularly in the Pauline epistles that proscribe how women's bodies should be covered (1 Timothy 2: 9–10, 1 Peter 3: 3–4), as well as the concern about the body and sexual (im)morality (1 Corinthians 6: 19–20 and Colossians 3: 5–14). In a similar way, this is also evoked in the gospels, through the warning to men about looking at women with lustful intent (Matthew 5:28).
4 With a specific reference to men as perpetrators of sexual violence, Abbey et al. (2004) demonstrate that the likelihood of a man committing sexual assault is increased with alcohol consumption as he becomes sexually disinhibited, has a heightened sexual arousability, and is increasingly impulsive.
5 The most recently available data pertaining to false accusations of rape in the UK is from the Crown Prosecution Service between 2011 and 2012, in which

35 prosecutions were made for false rape allegations, a very small number compared to rape allegation rates. Of course, there may be more cases that were not brought forward due to lack of evidence. Available: www.cps.gov.uk/sites/default/files/documents/publications/perverting_course_of_justice_march_2013.pdf.

6 However, Bergsma and Hahn further point out 'the imagery of the vineyard and wine is associated only with heterosexual intercourse in the Bible' (2005: 35). In addition to the three reasons they offer for Noah's outrage as I go on to discuss, they offer a fourth possible explanation: maternal incest. Referring to the ban of incest in Leviticus 20:11, 'the man who uncovers his father's wife has uncovered his father's nakedness', they argue that this can be read in conjunction with the text, with various commentators suggesting that Ham may have had incestual relations with Noah's wife, his mother. C. Wynand Retief (2010) also argues that it is a case of maternal incest, noting how 'in the background this is most probably a story of power struggles, of sons trying to usurp their father's authority and power' (2010: 797). Retief's argument would also stand for the act of paternal incest, however. Bergsma and Hahn note how the text follows the previous narrative in which Noah and his sons are commanded to 'be fruitful and multiply' (Genesis 9: 1, 7). In this view, Ham, like Lot's daughters, resorts to urgent incest in a quest to populate the earth, and in both cases, it is the fruits of the incestuous union and sexual assault who are punished, not the transgressors.

7 Frederick W. Bassett gives the following details on the debate as to whether Noah was castrated and by whom: 'A number of midrashim say that the offense involved the castration of Noah. Some say that Ham himself did the castrating. Others say that Ham's little son Canaan unmanned Noah by mischievously looping a cord about his genitals and drawing it tight. Ham's guilt in these accounts lies in the fact that he entered the tent, saw what had happened, and smilingly told his brothers. A sense of justice has obviously influenced the direction some of these midrashim have taken' (1971: 233).

8 In the United Kingdom, the National Society for the Prevention of Cruelty to Children (NSPCC) describe grooming as 'when someone builds a relationship, trust and emotional connection with a child or young person so they can manipulate, exploit and abuse them'. Available: www.nspcc.org.uk/what-is-child-abuse/types-of-abuse/grooming/.

9 Bal also uses the term 'reversed rape' in a previous commentary of Lot and his daughters (1992: 61). Conversely, Diane Sharon states how Bal 'does not note in the language and intertexts preceding it the suggestion of an attempted rape of Jael by Sisera' (2007: 255, fn 45). She states how 'the language and imagery flicker with both sexuality and deference against sexual aggression' (2007: 266).

10 For example, according to Stiebert (2019a: 6), *'innâ* is translated as rape in Genesis 34: 2, Judges 19: 24 and 20:5, 2 Samuel 13: 12, 14, 22 and 32, and Lamentations 5: 11. See Stiebert (2019a) and Gravett (2004) for comprehensive discussion of the verb.

11 Derks offers a significant footnote to exemplify his argument here, citing Smelik, 'because the phallus is a symbol and a signifier, no man can fully symbolize it. Although the patriarchal male subject has a privileged relation to the phallus, he will always fall short of the phallic ideal' (Smelik, 1998: 140; cited in Derks, 2015: 570). See also my discussion on 'Revisiting Male Theology: Having the Balls and the Fear of Impotency' in *Undoing Theology* (2018: 118–128).

12 Blyth continues, 'Reader and interpreters of the text who fill this enigmatic gap with assumptions about the duo's sexual dalliance are perhaps relying less on the textual evidence in Judges 16 than on those heteronormative sexual discourses dominant within their own sociocultural milieus' (2017: 61).

References

Abbey, Antonia, Philip O Buck, A. Monique Clinton and Tina Zawacki. 2004. 'Sexual Assault and Alcohol Consumption: What do we Know about their Relationship and What Types of Research are Still Needed?' *Aggression and Violent Behavior*, 9/3: 271–303.

Bailey, Randall. 1995. 'They're Nothing but Incestuous Bastards: The Polemic Use of Sex and Sexuality in Hebrew Canon Narratives'. In *Reading from this Place, Volume 1: Social Location and Biblical Interpretation in the United States*. Edited by Fernando F. Segovia and Mary A. Tolbert. Minneapolis: Fortress Press, pp. 121–138.

Bal, Mieke (trans. Matthew Gumpert). 1992. *Murder and Difference: Gender, Genre, and Scholarship on Sisera's Death*. Bloomington and Indianapolis: Indiana University Press.

Bassett, Frederick W. 1971. 'Noah's Nakedness and the Curse of Canaan, a Case of Incest?' *Vetus Testamentum*, 21/2: 232–237.

Bergsma, John Sietze and Scott Walker Hahn. 2005. 'Noah's Nakedness and the Curse on Caanan (Genesis 9: 20–27)'. *Journal of Biblical Literature*, 124/1: 25–40.

Blyth, Caroline. 2017. *Reimagining Delilah's Afterlives as Femme Fatale: The Lost Seduction*. London: Bloomsbury.

Brenner, Athalya. 1985. *The Israelite Woman: Social Role and Literary Type in Biblical Narrative*. London: Bloomsbury.

Carden, Michael. 1999a. 'Compulsory Heterosexuality in Biblical Narratives and their Interpretations: Reading Homophobia and Rape in Sodom and Gibeah'. *Australian Religion Studies Review*, 121: 47–60.

Carden, Michael. 1999b. 'Homophobia and Rape in Sodom and Gibeah: A Response to Ken Stone'. *Journal for the Study of the Old Testament*, 82: 83–96.

Carden, Michael. 2006. 'Genesis/Bereshit'. In *The Queer Bible Commentary*. Edited by Deryn Guest, Robert E. Goss, Mona West and Thomas Bohache. London: SCM Press, pp. 21–60.

Clines, David. 2015. 'The Scandal of a Male Bible'. The Ethel M. Wood Lecture for 2015, Kings College London. Available: www.academia.edu/10977758/The_Scandal_of_a_Male_Bible.

Clines, David. 2018. 'The Ubiquitous Language of Violence in the Hebrew Bible'. Paper presented at the Joint Meeting of Oudtestamentisch Werkgezelschap, Society for Old Testament Studies, and Old Testament Society of South Africa, Groningen, The Netherlands, 22 August 2019. Available: www.academia.edu/37260426/The_Ubiquitous_Language_of_Violence_in_the_Hebrew_Bible.

Crenshaw, James L. 1984. *A Whirlpool of Torment*. Philadelphia: Fortress Press.

Derks, Marco. 2015. '"If I Be Shaven, Then My Strength Will Go From Me" A Queer Reading of the Samson Narrative'. *Biblical Interpretation*, 23: 553–573.

Eilberg-Schwartz, Howard. 1994. *God's Phallus and Other Problems for Men and Monotheism*. Boston: Beacon Press.

Exum, J. Cheryl. 2016 [1993]. *Fragmented Women: Feminist Subversions of Biblical Narratives*. Second Edition. London: Bloomsbury.

Fewell, Danna Nolan and David M. Gunn. 1990. 'Controlling Perspectives: Women, Men, and the Authority of Violence in Judges 4 & 5'. *Journal of the American Academy of Religion*, 58/3: 389–411.

Fuchs, Esther. 2003. *Sexual Politics in the Biblical Narrative. Reading the Hebrew Bible as a Woman*. Sheffield: Sheffield Academic Press.

Gravett, Sandie. 2004. 'Reading "Rape" in the Hebrew Bible: A Consideration of Language'. *Journal for the Study of the Old Testament*, 28/3: 279–299.

Graybill, Rhiannon. 2016. *Are We Not Men? Unstable Masculinity in the Hebrew Prophets*. New York: Oxford University Press.

Greenough, Chris. 2018. *Undoing Theology: Life Stories from Non-normative Christians*. London: SCM Press.

Guest, Deryn. 2006. 'Judges'. In *The Queer Bible Commentary*. Edited by Deryn Guest, Robert E. Goss, Mona West and Thomas Bohache. London: SCM Press, pp. 167–189.

Harding, James E. 2018. 'Homophobia and Rape Culture in the Narratives of Early Israel'. In *Rape Culture, Gender Violence, and Religion: Biblical Perspectives*. Edited by Caroline Blyth, Emily Colgan and Katie B. Edwards. Cham: Palgrave Macmillan, pp. 159–178.

Hornsby, Teresa. 2007. *Sex Texts from the Bible: Selections Annotated and Explained*. Woodstock: Skylight Paths.

Jacob, Benno. 1934. *Das Erste Buch der Thora: Genesis*. Berlin: Schocken.

Javaid, Aliraza. 2019. 'What Support? Foucault, Power, and the Construction of Rape'. *Qualitative Sociology Review*, 151: 36–60.

Kessler, Martin and Karel Deurloo. 2004. *A Commentary on Genesis: The Book of Beginnings*. New York: Paulist Press.

Levinson, Joshua. 1997. 'An-Other Woman: Joseph and Potiphar's Wife. Staging the Body Politic'. *The Jewish Quarterly Review*, 873/4: 269–301.

Niditch, Susan. 1990. 'Samson As Culture Hero, Trickster, and Bandit: The Empowerment of the Weak'. *The Catholic Biblical Quarterly*, 52/4: 608–624.

Niditch, Susan. 2012. 'Genesis'. In *Women's Bible Commentary*. Edited by Carol A. Newsom, Sharon H. Ringe and Jacqueline E. Lapsley. Louisville: Westminster John Knox Press, pp. 27–45.

Phillips, Anthony. 1980. 'Uncovering the Father's Skirt'. *Vetus Testamentum*, 301: 38–43.

Pirson, Ron. 2004. 'The Twofold Message of Potiphar's Wife'. *Scandinavian Journal of the Old Testament*, 18/2: 248–259.

Reaves, Jayme R. 2016. *Safeguarding the Stranger: An Abrahamic Theology and Ethic of Protective Hospitality*. Cambridge: The Lutterworth Press.

Retief, C. Wynand. 2010. 'When Interpretation Traditions Speak Too Loud for Ethical Dilemmas to Be Heard: On the Untimely Death of Haran (Genesis 11: 28)'. *Old Testament Essays*, 23/3: 788–803.

Rowlett, Lori. 2001. 'Violent Femmes and S/M: Queering Samson and Delilah'. In *Queer Commentary and the Hebrew Bible*. Edited by Ken Stone. Sheffield: Sheffield Academic Press, pp. 106–115.

Satlow, Michael L. 1997. 'Jewish Constructions of Nakedness in Late Antiquity'. *Journal of Biblical Literature*, 1163: 429–454.

Scholz, Susanne. 2010. *Sacred Witness: Rape in the Hebrew Bible*. Minneapolis: Fortress Press.

Seifert, Elke. 1994. 'Lot und Seine Töchter: Eine Hermeneutik des Verdachts'. In *Feministische Hermeneutik und Erstes Testament: Analysen und Interpretationen*. Edited by Jahnow Hedwig. Stuttgart: Kohlhammer, pp. 48–65.

Sharon, Diane M. 2007. 'Choreography of an Intertextual Allusion to Rape in Judges 5: 24–27'. In *Brining the Hidden to Light: The Process of Interpretation. Studies in Honor Stephen A. Geller*. Edited by Kathryn F. Kravitz and Diane M. Sharon. Indiana: The Jewish Theological Seminary, pp. 249–269.

Smelik, Anneke. 1998. 'Gay and Lesbian Criticism'. In *The Oxford Guide to Film Studies*. Edited by John Hill and Pamela Church Gibson. Oxford: Oxford University Press, pp. 135–147.

Stiebert, Johanna. 2013. *Fathers and Daughters in the Hebrew Bible*. Oxford: Oxford University Press.

Stiebert, Johanna. 2019a. *Rape Myths, The Bible and #MeToo*. London: Routledge.

Stiebert, Johanna. 2019b. 'The Wife of Potiphar, Sexual Harassment, and False Rape Allegation'. In *The Bible and Gender Troubles in Africa*. Edited by Joachim Kügler, Rosinah Gabaitse and Johanna Stiebert. Bamberg: University of Bamberg Press, pp. 73–114.

Stone, Ken. 1996. *Sex, Honor, and Power in the Deuteronomistic History*. Sheffield: Sheffield Academic Press.

Stone, Ken. 2006. '1 and 2 Kings'. In *The Queer Bible Commentary*. Edited by Deryn Guest, Robert E. Goss, Mona West and Thomas Bohache. London: SCM Press, pp. 222–250.

von Rad, Gerhard. 1972. *Genesis*. Philadelphia: Westminster Press.

Yee, Gale A. 1993. 'By the Hand of a Woman: The Metaphor of the Woman Warrior in Judges 4'. *Semeia*, 61: 99–132.

3 Jesus too?

Introduction

This chapter attempts to probe the silence surrounding Jesus' enforced nudity in the gospel accounts of the crucifixion. Enforced nudity is, without doubt, sexual abuse. It has the strategy of shaming, humiliating, and disempowering its victim. In this chapter, I am not seeking to shock or to be indecent or offensive. Instead, the overarching aim of the chapter is, first, to explore some of the current literature around the labelling of Jesus' stripping and enforced nudity alongside the gospel accounts. The chapter then focusses on Jesus' embodiment, as I argue how the suppression of Jesus' sexuality is entangled with power dynamics of masculinities and patriarchy – in all of the biblical writings, as well as in the interpretations and theologies to which they have given rise. These power dynamics, moreover, are harmful not only to women, as many feminist commentators have amply demonstrated (Trible, 1984; Exum, 2016 [1993]), but also to men. The chapter explores what little is known about Jesus' embodiment as a Jewish male, including academic speculation on his assumed celibacy. In terms of what is generally asserted about Hebrew culture, celibacy appears to have been distinctly non-normative. Brief attention is then given to representations of Jesus in art, including depictions of his maleness, observing how the notion of a non-sexual Jesus is inextricably associated with purity, and consequently, this engenders reluctance to see his abuse as sexual. The chapter concludes by examining how the inability to recognise sexual abuse against men, including Jesus and in today's world, is connected to androcentrism and the male gaze.

'Behold the man' (John 19: 5)

The master narrative of Christianity emerges out of the world's most popular story of excruciating abuse: the crucifixion. The passion scenes described in the gospels narrate episodes of crippling physical violence and emotional abuse towards Jesus at the hands of the Roman authorities. The crucifixion renders Jesus involuntarily nude. Michael Trainor notes that, at the crucifixion, 'Jesus is not only subject to physical abuse. . . . He is now subject to sexual abuse. The exposure of his penis, the symbol of sexual power and identity, is the ultimate act of shaming and abuse' (2014: 148).[1]

The accounts of Jesus' forced stripping vary slightly from gospel to gospel. In Matthew, we read an account of Jesus' trial and crucifixion where the high priest tears Jesus' clothes (26: 65); the soldiers strip him and put a scarlet robe on him to mock him (27: 28). They then take off the robe and put Jesus' own clothes back on him (27: 31). When he has been crucified, Jesus' clothes are divided up (27: 35), indicating his nudity at the time of crucifixion. Indeed, Trainor highlights that there is often no mention of Jesus' nudity because 'nudity would have been presumed' (2014: 25). In Mark's gospel, there is no mention of the high priest tearing Jesus' clothes; Jesus is forced to wear a purple robe while he is mocked by the soldiers (15: 17), and then they put his own clothes back on him, which suggests that his clothes had already been forcibly removed (15: 20). Jesus' clothes are then divided up in verse 24. Luke's gospel also notes how Jesus is dressed in an elegant robe (23: 11), but there is no mention of the stripping that would precede this. Following his crucifixion, his clothes are (again) divided up (23: 34). In John's gospel, Jesus is flogged, and soldiers dress him in a purple robe and put a crown of thorns on his head (19: 1–2); Pilate brings Jesus out, saying 'Behold the man!' (19: 5). Following the crucifixion, his clothes are divided up among the four soldiers, and they draw lots to get his tunic, described as 'seamless, woven in one piece from top to bottom' (19: 23).[2] Indeed, the gospel accounts of the passion form part of the Christian devotions The Stations of the Cross, where station ten focusses on the scene where Jesus is stripped of his clothes.

The shame and stigma associated with Jesus' nudity echoes the discussion of involuntary nudity and stripping in the Hebrew Bible, in Chapter 2. Along with the shame of enforced nudity, victims of crucifixion in the Roman world of the first century CE would likely have suffered other indignities (Trainor, 2014), including involuntary defecation, swelling of the penis, and penile discharge. Martin Hengel, in his examination of crucifixion in the ancient world, observes the scandal of the cross: 'By the public display of a naked victim at a prominent place . . . crucifixion also represents his uttermost humiliation' (1977: 87). Hengel references Deuteronomy 21: 23 to highlight how the crucifixion would have been seen as particularly shameful to Jesus' followers, given their Jewish heritage: 'you must not leave the body hanging on the pole overnight. Be sure to bury it that same day, because anyone who is hung on a pole is under God's curse'.

As Trainor notes, the scene is one where the abuse is physical, emotional, sexual, and public:

> Everything associated with crucifixion totally degraded and abused its victim: public trial, compulsory march to the place of execution, carrying the cross beam, confiscation of clothing and forced nudity, physical mutilation, being impaled or transfixed to the beam of sometimes quirky and comical crosses, the entertainment this provided for onlookers, physical deformation, loss of bodily control, enlargement of the penis, breaking of limbs to hasten lingering death and, finally, denial of an honourable burial as the corpse became the food for scavenging animals and carrion birds.
>
> (2014: 24)

Elaine Heath offers a similar reading of the gospel accounts of Jesus' nudity. She notes how interpreting the enforced nudity as sexual shaming is not anachronistic, as enforced public nudity was considered an act of sexual violence in Jesus' time and culture:

> In Jesus's culture, as in Middle Eastern cultures today, to be stripped naked in front of a watching crowd was an act of sexual violation. . . . The torture was sadistic, carried out while he was naked in order to maximize his humiliation in front of the voyeuristic crowd. Like a child victim of rape or a victim in snuff porn, Jesus was pinned down, bound, violated, penetrated, torn.
>
> (2011: 123)

At his trial, Jesus is reported to have been silent in response to his accusers, despite knowing the fate that lay ahead of him (Matthew 27: 12, Mark 15: 5, Luke 23: 9). One of the main theological questions that emerges from engagement with these gospel accounts is: why did Jesus not speak out? Jesus' silence is often interpreted as dignified, stoic, and even heroic.[3] Marcella Althaus-Reid notes how 'Jesus was constructed in a way such that he was born to speak and to be silent at the same time' (2000: 107). Jesus does not speak out against his own abusers, yet elsewhere in the gospels he calls out injustices. Silence operates around sexual violence against men today. Despite the huge contrasts in the cultural contexts from the ancient Jewish and Greco-Roman settings to today, silence around male victimisation is scaffolded by hegemonic masculinity and has been passed on through millennia. There is a culture of silence that surrounds victims of sexual violence, described by Sarah Caprioli and David A. Crenshaw as a 'the silent bond' (2017: 191). They attribute this silence to the intimate and internalised nature of sexual abuse; as they state, 'sexual abuse is an intimate wound to both the spirit and body, often shrouded in the trilogy of shame, secrecy, and stigma' (2017: 191). Although they are writing in the broader discipline of human psychology, Caprioli and Crenshaw's argument is illuminating and can be extended to the interpretations of Jesus' silence during his trials. Where there is an imbalance of power, a victim may feel a sense of safety in remaining silent, using this in an effort not to provoke their abusers further. Jesus' silence is therefore less a sign of his heroic stoicism, as Craig Keener posits (2009), and rather simply a means by which he attempted to pacify his captors, or a genuine sense of fear. Deeming silence as heroic is problematic, as it discourages victims from speaking out about their abuse and against their abusers.[4] Yet, the victim is not the only one who chooses or is forced to be silent by their abuser, but the denial of abuse by onlookers can also lead to victims' silence. In this way, I argue that Jesus is further silenced by those who refuse to see him as a victim of sexual abuse.

Even though the gospel accounts are clear that Jesus was publicly humiliated and sexually shamed, literal readings have not been sufficient and Jesus' own victimisation has been hidden and silenced in Christian thought and traditions (Trainor, 2014; Tombs, 2018 [1999]). It is time for Jesus' sexual abuse to be taken seriously. The shame and stigma surrounding male abuse can be mapped onto the gospel accounts of Jesus' own sexual victimisation. To conceive of Jesus as a victim of sexual abuse would result in the same appropriation of shame narratives noted in Chapter 1. Jesus as a victim is disempowered, emasculated, and exposed. Indeed, shame and stigma function to depict a male victim of sexual abuse as 'feminised', playing to the myth that only women can be sexually abused. Consequently, Katie Edwards and David Tombs observe that women are identified as sexual, and therefore their abuse is more readily recognised:

> Sexual abuse doesn't form part of the narrative of masculinity inherent in representations of Jesus. Naked women, however, are immediately identified as sexual objects. Seeing a woman being forcibly stripped, then, might be more recognisable as sexual abuse than the stripping of Jesus in the Gospels of Matthew and Mark. If Christ was a female figure we wouldn't hesitate to recognise her ordeal as sexual abuse.
> (2018)[5]

The same social scripts of silence, shame, and stigma alongside myths about sexual violence against men all prevent us from thinking about Jesus as a victim of sexual violence. Moreover, no religions, or at least no followers of a faith, want to perceive their deity as disempowered, emasculated, and exposed. Jayme Reaves and David Tombs detail how research in this area has been met with some ambivalent responses:

> The stigma and expected loss of respect may be why the statement that Jesus was a victim of sexual abuse is often fiercely resisted. The operating assumption appears to be that, if it were true, it would lower Jesus in the eyes of decent people. Respectable church members wish to defend Jesus from such a fate, and to protect the Christian faith from such a concession.
>
> (2019: 23)

Equally then, if such respectable church members see a devaluation of Jesus because of his status as a victim of sexual abuse, then surely that reveals their distaste for all victims, as people who are damaged, sullied, and maybe even blameworthy. The distaste for Jesus as a victim of sexual violence is also grounded in the myth that men should *not* be victims of sexual violence, and that if Jesus is a victim, his masculinity is undermined. In other words, if Jesus is a victim, he is betraying hegemonic masculinity, and this poses a real threat to patriarchy. Thus, not only is there a need to recognise masculinities as plural and diverse, there is an urgent need to dismantle the very social and cultural scripts and narratives that underpin hegemonic masculinity; it is toxic, and it sustains gendered violence. Rather than take a monolithic view of men and their association with patriarchy and hegemonic masculinity, we must recognise diversity in men's masculinities – just as Jesus subverted expectations of masculine ideals, not only through his passion and death, but also through his relationships and interactions with women during his ministry.[6]

Tombs (2018 [1999]) and Reaves and Tombs (2019) argue that the naming of Jesus as a victim of sexual abuse may help churches deal more effectively with the recent clergy sexual abuse scandals it has failed to address adequately. Reaves and Tombs (2019) maintain that acknowledging Jesus' sexual abuse has the potential to open up new conversations about sexual abuse in the churches. They envisage that this, in turn, will allow for attitudes of shame and stigma around sexual violence to be examined, and they offer a practical example of an encounter between a congregation and a survivor:

> In some cases, a survivor might be the target of gossip or rumour. In other cases, the negative attitude comes through the silence. If a church never speaks of sexual violence, nor acknowledges those who have suffered from it, it can seem that the church does not want to know about it, and that the experiences of survivors are unimportant. When

the experiences of survivors are never addressed in church, it is easy for survivors to take this as a message that there is something wrong with them. Either what they did (victim blaming), or what they have become (victim stigmatising), or both, makes them unworthy in the eyes of respectable church members.

(Reaves and Tombs, 2019: 23)

Reaves and Tombs contend that effective pastoral responses can be found in reading the passion narratives that recognise the abuse against Jesus depicted therein. As they state:

Naming Jesus as a victim of sexual abuse therefore matters far more than is obvious at first. It is not just getting the historical record correct, it can make a real difference to how survivors see themselves and how they are perceived and treated by others.

(Reaves and Tombs, 2019: 25)

Nonetheless, they state, 'this assumption is not to suggest that the churches should only think sexual abuse is important if Jesus was a victim. Sexual abuse should be a concern for the churches regardless of who is experiencing it' (2019: 22)

In a similar quest to gain constructive pastoral responses to the sexual abuse scandals that beset the Catholic Church, Trainor discusses the relevance of the gospel accounts today. Trainor suggests that 'the story of Jesus is fundamental to a church that seeks to discern how it is to act and respond authentically in this difficult and scandalous moment' (2014: 6). Trainor offers three significant examples for how churches are able to do this. The first involves examining how Peter's denial and Judas' betrayal of Jesus can offer a warning against silencing anything seen as scandalous. Second, Trainor encourages performance-based readings of the passion narratives, to facilitate engagement with how the gospel accounts speak to the present. Trainor's third example of how the recognition of Jesus' sexual abuse can encourage pastoral responses is in the way that it invites reflection on the abuse of power in church leadership and encourages church leaders to respond sensitively to those who have been abused.

Trainor (2014), Tombs (2018[1999]), and Reaves and Tombs (2019) thus draw explicit parallels between the abuse of Jesus to the abuse of contemporary victims; they also demonstrate the pressing need for effective pastoral responses by churches and authorities to deal more effectively with sexual violence against men. Their approach may therefore form a strategy that offers important practical methods for the churches' handling of abuse. In a similar manner, the notion of Jesus as a co-sufferer with marginalised groups, especially the poor and oppressed, is one of the motifs of liberation theology, especially those emerging in Latin American contexts. Sharing in Jesus' suffering is also a theological trope that appears in practical theological literature pertaining to trauma. Ruard Ganzevoort (2008) explores shame and stigma associated with sexual abuse against men and describes how focussing on a religious narrative helps abuse survivors make sense of their lives. Describing the familial abuse experienced by a Roman Catholic man who found healing in the thought of Jesus' own suffering at the hands of his father, Ganzevoort notes how the path from stigmata to survival is one of faith and prayer. For sufferers of abuse, 'devotional life gave them the opportunity to attribute spiritual meaning to the suffering they had endured and to symbolize their traumatization in the development of stigmata' (2008: 24–25). Yet, elsewhere, Ganzevoort also notes that 'many, especially male victims, would rather deny these experiences, omit them from their core narratives, or reinterpret them so that they are no longer perceived as abuse' (2001: 55). There is clearly no universal response to the issue of sexual violence against men, as victims develop their own, unique ways of coping. While some may appreciate and benefit from the motif of Jesus as a victim who shares their trauma, for others, this may not be helpful. For those who have found solace in Jesus as a victim through their own spiritual lives, the #JesusToo movement on social media has provided as a valuable platform for Christian survivors of abuse.

#JesusToo?

The #JesusToo movement is certainly not as well known as the #MeToo or #ChurchToo phenomena. Emerging alongside #ChurchToo, #JesusToo has been used by people to identify and label Jesus' own suffering as violent abuse. Indeed, female figures who suffered rape in the Bible have also appeared through the hashtag phenomenon, including #TamarToo (2 Samuel 13) and #DinahToo (Genesis 34). But #JesusToo has been used in several different ways, some of which move away from its origins in uncovering the silence and stigma surrounding abuse. #JesusToo has been used by Christians to tell abuse survivors that Jesus has shared their pain, and that through faith in Jesus they can receive healing. Some users of #JesusToo have sought to inform survivors of sexual violence that Jesus knows all about their abuse and they can turn to him in prayer. #JesusToo has therefore been aimed at those who have experienced abuse or felt silenced, shamed, vulnerable, or oppressed; it recalls the centrality of Christian hope of victory over suffering and sin found in Jesus' sacrifice and redemption.

Even where #JesusToo is used to preach, convert, proselytise, or offer a rebranded form of contemporary Christianity, it recognises the social and cultural need to respond to gendered violence, rape culture, and toxic masculinity. It seeks to examine contemporary issues with ancient ones, given the continued significance of the Bible in today's world. This is a step in the right direction, as it begins to dismantle misogyny, patriarchy, and hegemonic masculinity from within the Christian tradition itself.

Notwithstanding, there remain obstacles that render the #JesusToo movement both limited and problematic for those who wish to draw comparisons between Jesus' experience of sexual abuse and the experience of contemporary survivors. While this section so far has detailed the connections between Jesus' own suffering and endurance of sexual violence in the passion narratives, one limitation of the biblical texts is that there are no insights into Jesus' emotional and psychological responses to his abuse as it occurs, or in the immediate aftermath. Trainor himself sees the limitations of using the gospel narratives in any attempt to mirror contemporary experiences of sexual abuse. He expresses concerns against any theology of suffering or trauma that erroneously interprets the gospels as describing Jesus as emotionally strong and in any way consenting to receive his abuse and suffering. Trainor remarks how contemporary victims 'would recoil from such a Jesus who appears strong and embraces, or even encourages, victimization' (2014: 9). Moreover, Jesus' abuse was a one-off event, whereas sexual assaults can be repeated over a sustained period of time: the duration and frequency of abuse, age at the onset of abuse, relationship to the offender, and the nature of the abuse are all significant factors that impact on disclosure and recovery (Romano and De Luca, 2001). The gospels share the brutality and violence of Jesus' physical, emotional, and sexual violations, yet Jesus was delivered from his abuse relatively quickly by his heavenly father. That being so, Trainor notes, 'the divine power accessible to Jesus seems inaccessible to ordinary human beings and especially the abused' (2014: 10). Jesus' situation therefore contrasts against the emotional and psychological impact that so often follows abuse survivors. Thus, Trainor himself is aware of the limitations of finding comfort in Jesus as a co-sufferer. While the gospels offer reflection and insight about Jesus' own abuse, each reader and each victim of sexual abuse will bring their own thoughts and responses to this. Most importantly, however, shedding light on Jesus' abuse undoubtedly offers serious contemplation about sexual violence to theology, biblical studies, and the churches.

Another issue raised by the #JesusToo movement is that some people feel disquiet about Jesus' status as a victim of sexual violence because this puts emphasis on his sexed body. Jesus' humanity is fully depicted in his representation as a victim of sexual violence, yet his violation has been obfuscated and the silence has stood for more than two thousand years. One of the reasons that the portrayal of Jesus as a victim of sexual violence is so polemic is that Jesus, generally, is presented as non-sexual – in the scriptures and in the Christian tradition. Regarding Jesus' sexuality specifically, Lisa Isherwood comments:

> we know nothing about the sex life of Jesus and this silence has, in traditional theology, been taken to mean that he did not have one, but it is not too hard to understand why this line of thought does not really stand the test of reason.
>
> (2018: 277)

Isherwood refers to the emphasis on normative marriage, sexuality, and procreation as central to Jewish beliefs. In Christian theology, the equation that sexuality exemplifies the humanity of Jesus is observed by several scholars (Phipps, 1973; Nelson, 1979; Le Donne, 2013) and the very same attention given to Jesus' sexuality and humanity should also be given to envisaging him as a victim. In the introduction to *Embodiment* (1979), James Nelson tells the story about the attempt by Jens Jorgen Thorsen to make a film about the sex life of Jesus (1979: 11–12). The film caused outraged responses, including one reported to be from the Queen of England, who found the idea 'obnoxious' (Nelson, 1979: 12). At the time, the Bishop of Wakefield said the following: 'If he was other than a fully human being then, for me "the Word becoming flesh" is not wholly true . . . Jesus was no stranger to sex and its problems' (cited in Nelson, 1979: 12). As seen earlier, the very fact that Jesus is associated with sex causes outrage and reveals a Christology that emphasises Jesus' purity and therefore deprecates sex as sinful or sullied. This idea further speaks back to a resistance and an unwillingness to conceive of Jesus' own sexual abuse. In the following section, I explore further the discernible associations between the hiddenness of Jesus' sex and the blindness to his sexual abuse.

Problematics in representing Jesus' sex and sexuality

The inability or refusal to recognise Jesus' sexual abuse could also stem from the mystery that surrounds his sex and sexuality. There is a distinction in the presentation of God the Father, God the Son as undoubtedly male, and therefore sexed, yet God is non-sexual. The Christian tradition has fetishised sexual purity, including that belonging to Jesus. Jesus' sex is clearly depicted as male in the New Testament: he is the *Son* of God, for instance, and according to one gospel account he undergoes the Jewish rite of circumcision (Luke 2: 21). But while he has a *sex*, any reference to Jesus' *sexuality* is virtually erased in much of the New Testament and most of Christian theology.[7] Where it does receive cautious mention, however, he is presumed to be heterosexual; he is described as the bridegroom in relation to the bride, for instance in John 3: 29.[8] Indeed, if the bride of Christ is the church, then hegemonic masculinity also poses problems for male believers who worship a male God.

Eilberg-Schwartz works within the Jewish tradition and problematises the interactions between 'the love of a male human for a male God' (1994: 10), exploring the themes of homoeroticism and how taking the position of devotee results in a perceived feminisation of men. He draws parallels with the framing of Christ's body as problematic for Christian men, as Paul's letter to the Ephesians calls for multiple submissions: wife to husband, husband to wife, and the church to Christ. As Christ is male, then the church has theologically been described as female, including the use of female pronouns in doctrines and positional statements. For men to be part of the church, they are drawn into the position of wife of Christ (Ephesians 5: 21). This is similar to passages in the Hebrew Bible where Israel is illustrated as the wife of Yahweh (Jeremiah 2:23–5:19 and Ezekiel 16). Both positions result in a dilemma for male believers in monotheistic faiths where the divine is male. The idea of men being in a relationship with a male deity is not solely historical and still raises problematic responses today. In one example, Stephen Finley examines the conflict for Black heterosexual Christian men being drawn into a relationship with God that has same-sex overtones and 'phallic anxiety', observing through his ethnographic study 'the underlying homophobic anxiety of some men, not only with the possibility of symbolic entry by a dominant male divinity, but also with ostensible hatred and disdain for male homosexuals' (2007: 319). Finley observes the absence of men from a Baptist church in the USA, noting specifically how worship of a male God is problematic for Black heterosexual men as this 'places the male in the "feminine" or passive recipient position of the relationship' (2007: 317).

Here I distinguish between Jesus' *sex* (as reportedly male), and his *sexuality*, a concept which encompasses any discussion of his capacity for feelings, thoughts, attractions, behaviours, and intimacy with others. Following Kinsey et al. (1953, 1948), sexuality is not bipartite, but fluid. Avoidance of Jesus' sexuality has the effect of rendering him – like the ideal devotee and later the ideal priest and nun – as asexual or, at the very least, celibate. In 1 Corinthians 7: 8, Paul advises against marriage for those who are unmarried and widowed, while in the Jewish imagination, sexual activity was encouraged through its explicit connection to procreation through God's commandment in Genesis 1: 28, 'Be fruitful and increase in number; fill the earth and subdue it', repeated in Genesis 9: 1, 7. In early Roman times, there were even penalties against celibacy, yet it became a sacred vow in Orthodox and Catholic traditions, denoting a devotee's detachment from the physical and material world in favour of a spiritual relationship with God. Hence, Robert Beckford notes a cherished impulse to see Jesus as a man who is sexually pure:

> The biblical text tells us very little about Jesus' sexuality. Consequently, much of European church scholarship has tended to represent him as a celibate man and a model for a life of devotion . . . it is no surprise that . . . today, all icons, paintings and sculptures of Jesus cover his genitals, inferring that he was or is non-sexual.
>
> (1996: 17)

Few exceptions to visual representations of a nude adult Jesus exist, such as the contemporary work of artist Ed Knippers, who depicts nude representations of Jesus and other biblical characters in his paintings,[9] as well as representations of a nude Christ in ancient art (Steinberg, 1996 [1983]). These works of art inevitably raise hostile reactions or are deemed controversial. There are direct tensions between art and religion, and vice-versa. In reference to Knippers' work, Rondall Reynoso comments that 'many in the evangelical world equate nudity with pornography and, as such, have stood in opposition to his work' (2013: 11).

As noted earlier, a male deity can be problematic for male believers who have anxieties around homosexuality. The heavenly father is male, but non-sexual, in the dominant Christian tradition, an observation critically evidenced by Rita Gross:

> the traditional image of deity, God the Father, the God of our fathers, is a non-sexual symbol. We have already seen how possible it is to have a concept of a theistic Ultimate that is so exalted above all sexuality. In fact, God has been exalted above male sexuality only.
>
> (1983: 236)

In a similar vein, the hiddenness of God's body has been examined by Howard Eilberg-Schwartz (1994) and Johanna Stiebert (2016). Eilberg-Schwartz focusses on the divine cover-up of God's body, including the hiddenness of the divine penis, while Stiebert reflects upon how 'divine corporeality becomes increasingly veiled and obscured' (2016: 26). Her argument demonstrates how, over time, there is an emphasis on God's voice rather than God's body in the Hebrew Bible. God becomes less visible and more auditory, which diffuses any potential controversies surrounding the imagination of God's body.

In Christian theology, in fact, this idea of non-sexuality is a family affair, as not only is Jesus rendered asexual in the Bible, his earthly parents are, too.

Given the ideology of a non-sexual God and Jesus, Mary and Joseph's absent sexualities also serve to confer purity and holiness onto them. The focus on Mary's virginity in church doctrines, particularly in Roman Catholicism, testify to the negative religious attitudes towards sexuality, where sex is defiling and sinful. This is evidenced in doctrines relating to her own immaculate conception, the immaculate conception of Jesus and the assumption of the virgin. The fact Joseph did not have sex with Mary (Matthew 1: 18–23) also invites interpretation to the idea of celibacy, although in Matthew 1: 25, we are told that Joseph did not consummate his marriage with Mary *until* she gave birth to Jesus, a note which may contest the idea that Mary remained a virgin throughout her life. Certainly, Mary is presented as a virgin when pregnant with Jesus, but it is ambiguous if she remained a virgin for life after Jesus' birth. Although the Bible does not enter into detail about Joseph's age, there is speculation that he was a very old man based on the fact that he is mentioned in the gospels for the last time when Jesus was 12 years of age during the annual Passover visit to the temple (Luke 2: 41–51). Unlike his wife Mary, Joseph does not appear anywhere else in the gospels, nor is he present at the crucifixion.

In light of this discussion, it is clear that traditional Christian theology has set boundaries on the concept of incarnation. The radical theological concept of God becoming flesh is therefore diluted by a Christian tradition unable or unwilling to shed light on what it means to be fully human. If a focus on Jesus' sexuality is something that provokes scandal or outrage, this reveals much about the boundaries of our thinking about the human body and about sexuality. Nelson suggests that the Christian commitment to proclaiming the humanity of God is tested when one takes issue with Jesus' sexuality. He states, 'if we are offended at the thought that Jesus was ever inclined toward a fully sexual union, such offense might simply betray the suspicion that sex is unworthy of the Savior because it is unworthy of us' (1979: 76). Nelson is right, therefore, to connect the repugnance of imagining Jesus as sexual to Christian attitudes towards sex in general.

Scholars debating Jesus' sexuality often hypothesise about his marital status as evidence of his (hetero)sexuality (Phipps, 1973; Satlow, 2001). Moreover, exploring the possibilities of Jesus' sexuality reaffirms his status as human and, therefore, victim. Searching for some representation of Jesus' sexuality is a task clouded in taboo, just as any discussion of sexual violence against men is similarly off-limits. My intention here is to spotlight his sexuality in ancient contexts, examining how cultural scripts relating to sexuality and expectations of men can cast light on his sexual abuse as depicted in the gospels. The first cultural script relating to the male sexuality of an adult Jesus relates to speculation about his marital status. William Phipps, in detailing the rites of passage for a Jewish man, highlights how it was customary for a man to marry. Given the silence in the gospels about Jesus' marriage, Phipps demonstrates how marriage was part of male maturation, arranged by a Jewish father (1973). He states, 'deviations from normative behavior are likely to be remembered and thus lodged in oral and written traditions, so it makes sense to assume that Jesus and his apostles were all circumcised and married' (1973: 45). The gospels narrate deliberate subversions of conventions of the time, including Jesus' own (critical) words on family in Luke 14: 26, so it would be surprising to have not documented any defiance of the convention of marriage.

Continuing with a focus on Jesus' sexuality through the lens of marriage, Michael Satlow (2001) examines sources from Palestine and Babylonia and observes how in Palestine at the time, the average age for men to marry was around 30, usually to women 10 or 15 years younger. William Loader (2005) builds on these arguments to suggest that Jesus may not have had the option of marriage, given that his crucifixion and death occurred in his early thirties. Loader's view is that if Jesus had been married, as was the norm, he would certainly have had children, too, as that was just as much an expectation of Jewish men. For Loader, the fact that the gospels do not name or make reference to any spouse or offspring make it unlikely that Jesus was a father or a husband. Referring to the radical nature of his life and ministry, Loader concludes that Jesus was unmarried by choice rather than default: 'on balance, it is more probable that Jesus was not married, and this was a matter of choice not accident' (2005: 144). Speculations on whether Jesus was conventional but did not get around to marrying, or whether he was killed before he could marry, serve to raise questions about Jesus' own subversion of masculinity and patriarchal expectations of marriage and procreation. For Christian theology, this is a double-edged sword. On the one hand, if Jesus' being married is suggestive of Jesus having sex, the theological trope of celibacy is problematised. On the other hand, if Jesus is not married, this leads to contemporary interpretations that he may not be heterosexual, and likewise this troubles Christian theology. Both questions rupture traditional theological interpretations. Furthermore, the silence around Jesus' sexuality within the Christian tradition is one of the reasons there is a deafening silence about his sexual abuse. It requires us to contravene expectations about Jesus' sexual purity and look upon his nakedness. To be a victim of sexual abuse would, for some Christians, undoubtedly tarnish the tradition of Jesus' purity. In Chapter 2, I explored how male rape was too terrifying to narrate, and how myths about male victims of sexual violence in contemporary contexts were actually at play in the biblical texts. Because of hegemonic masculinity, homophobia, and misogyny, there is a fear of being feminised as victim. Therefore, the shame and stigma around sexual violence against men has led to its silence. In turn, my examination of Jesus' own abuse leads us to see how Jesus represented the male victim so effortfully avoided in the Hebrew scriptures.

The divine penis: purity, power, potency

Beyond hypothetical considerations of Jesus' sexuality based on the culture of ancient times, Leo Steinberg's comprehensive critique of representations of Jesus' penis in Renaissance art showcases a number of images of a nude Jesus, including pictures of Madonna and Child where the infant is often nude, alongside fewer images of a nude adult where the genitalia are veiled by a cloth or Jesus' own strategically placed hand (1996 [1983]). With this in mind, Lisa Isherwood and Dirk von der Horst comment how Jesus' genitals were a focus of adoration in the fifteenth century:

> The traditional reason given for this is that Jesus did not sin and so even his genitals are to be adored. . . . If a naked Jesus has been difficult to deal with over the years then one with an erect penis has caused even more problems. Renaissance art does not even avoid that awkward scenario and shows both the Christ child and Jesus the man with an erect penis. When the child is shown the symbolism is that of potency in relation to the later life of celibacy; one without the other was considered to be of no use to a saviour.
>
> (2018: 17)

In his cultural history of the penis, David Friedman also picks up on the adoration of the infant Jesus' genitalia, by observing how the admiration of his genitalia is representative of his sinless form. He highlights how the infant Jesus is uncircumcised in the majority of these paintings, despite the gospel reference to his circumcision in Luke 2: 21. He speculates that European artists would have preferred to depict the penis in its original form, and that anti-Semitism played a role in this. Friedman states, 'it proved that the penis of the new Adam was born without sin and, even more to the point, without the shame the Church says the rest of us feel on our genitalia' (2001: 51). Friedman also extends his discussion to the history of Jesus' foreskin as a prized religious relic (2001: 52–54).

Nonetheless, widespread Christian iconography depicting an adult Jesus at the crucifixion uses a loincloth to cover up any representation of Jesus' manhood, denoting how the adult male is more readily sexualised. Jesus' penis is symbolic of power and potency, and his forced nudity and exposure represent an undoing of this power and potency, resulting in the ultimate disgrace for a man.[10] In art, the suffering and crucified Jesus is almost always covered up in order to avoid illustrating this moment of powerlessness. Regarding this theme, Steinberg remarks how in the fifteenth century, crucifixes did begin to appear in which Jesus had clearly marked genitalia. He gives the example from the Donatello School, where two examples are shown – one with a loincloth, and another without, after restoration (1996 [1983]: 136). Steinberg's extensive portfolio of images offers examples from three presentations of Maerten van Heemskerck's *Man of Sorrows* (1996 [1983]: 87–89), yet in some examples, even when Jesus is covered with a loincloth, his genitalia are still represented as an outline that can be seen under the cloth.[11] This is particularly noted in the work of 1532 where Jesus' penis is covered with a loincloth but its contours are graphically visible. The circumcised penis, a reminder of Jesus' maleness and Jewishness, is enlarged, representing its engorgement during the crucifixion. Steinberg describes the image as 'an outrageous conception' (1996 [1983]: 86). He further expands on this, commenting how 'Heemskerck's iconic vision transgresses because (for most of us) the pictorial economy is thrown off balance by the genital impact' (1996 [1983]: 90). Steinberg states how a viewer either misses it, or sees nothing else.

While Steinberg's speculation on viewers' responses may be true, it is important to be aware of how the representation of the penis here is symbolic of the shame and powerlessness of Jesus, the emasculated rabbi. This contrasts sharply with the cultural imaginations of the penis and its association with power, strength, and vigour. Exposure of genitalia was part of the shaming and stigma associated with crucifixion, so there is an absolute accuracy to Heemskerck's portrayal even under the loincloth, despite outraged responses including from Steinberg himself. Images offering any visual representation of a nude Jesus, such as those explored by Steinberg, do not appear in churches and are not popular in religious iconography. Rather, images depicting the physical suffering of Jesus in agonising pain, cut, tortured, bleeding, and bruised are prolific in art and theology, while the notion that Jesus' body was also sexually violated is impermissible. It reveals much more about religion, society, and culture that a penis is considered more taboo than a beaten, broken, and abused body.

In recognising the control such images have on Christian history and thought, Isherwood draws attention to the way in which the early church recognised the power of sex and its relationship to morality. From early on, the church created rules and laws that serve to regulate and control it:

> The Church Fathers took the lived reality of Jesus of Nazareth and turned it into the body of Christ. The enfleshed first-century rabbi became the virginal and celibate Son of God whose perfect body was

taken up to heaven in its completeness. It is this body that has exercised massive control over the bodies of the faithful for generations.

(Isherwood, 2018: 277)

Jesus' and Mary's body are sites on which the Christian regulation of the human body are placed. Therefore, the consequences of configuring Jesus as a victim of sexual abuse are theologically and politically perilous, as they place into question the very purity codes which regulate Christian views on embodiment. Thus, through the representation of Jesus as a victim of sexual abuse, the perfect body is rendered imperfect; it is violated and disempowered and therefore unable to exercise control over other bodies, as it has done throughout Christian history and theology. In her work on cultural representations of the penis, Elizabeth Stephens comments how 'the specificity of the physical penis is obscured by a phallic ideal' (2007: 85). Jesus' penis itself is shrouded in mystery, while its importance in upholding traditional Christian ideals about purity is ubiquitous. The focus on the penis therefore allows for a move away from unrealistic attitudes about purity towards a realisation that embodiment is messy. This is equally true for hegemonic masculinity. Rather than being conceived as a rigid form of compulsory behaviour for men, demystifying the penis serves to demystify phallocentrism, allowing for masculinities that are less toxic and more fluid and flaccid. Here, I agree with Stephens, who argues, 'no longer the metonym for a rigid and unyielding masculinity, the phallic body here has opened its borders to the ecstatic effects of its own fluidity' (2007: 96).

Moreover, there is a real anxiety around the embodiment of male sexuality itself. In his book *God's Phallus and Other Problems for Men and Monotheism* (1994), Eilberg-Schwartz picks up on similar themes, describing how the assumption that God is male is loaded. There is a contradiction between God's maleness and his masculinity: God is depicted as non-sexual, yet God's maleness confers privileges onto men. Eilberg-Schwartz notes, 'God is a masculine deity whose maleness is repressed and avoided' (1994: 25). With the aim of examining critically the perceived stability of the connection between masculinity and the penis, Eilberg-Schwartz writes how 'the conflation of masculinity and maleness makes the image of a masculine God appear to authorize male sexuality more than it actually does' (1994: 25). Eilberg-Schwartz draws on the work of Jacques Lacan in demonstrating how it is the phallus that is symbolic of patriarchy rather than the actual penis itself. As the phallus is 'veiled', according to Eilberg-Schwartz, this is also problematic for men:

> To be like God the creator, they must procreate. But to be like God they should have no sex and no desire. It is a crucial question, then, to

consider why divine masculinity is figured without desire and without its potent symbol, the phallus.

(1994: 26)

The distinction between the penis and the phallus requires some careful attention, as the notion of Lacan's phallus provides a further move away from Jesus' embodiment, similar to the idea of Jesus as celibate and non-sexual. The debate about the phallus as symbolic of patriarchy and Jesus' penis is taken up by Althaus-Reid in *Indecent Theology* (2000). She is less concerned with what is revealed biblically or theologically about Jesus' actual biological sex and more concerned with how Jesus' gender is used to uphold patriarchal, androcentric, and heteronormative theologies:

> it may be acceptable to look at a nude Jesus hanging tortured on the cross as long as he doesn't have an erect penis. Of course, we don't know if Jesus had an erect penis at his death; for all we know, we cannot even take for granted that he had a penis at all. . . . We read that Jesus had a penis when he was taken to be circumcised (Luke 2:21), but we don't know if it developed, if he had an accident, three testicles or grew up with what might be considered a socially underdeveloped penis, and so forth. In other words, we know more about the process of gender making of the man Jesus than of his biological status, or, what is more important, his sexuality.
>
> (Althaus-Reid, 2000: 104)[12]

In asking such indecent theological questions, Althaus-Reid does not shy away from thinking about Jesus' penis; rather, she denotes it has little importance for Christian theology.[13] In this way, the biblical trace we have of Jesus' actual penis pales in significance compared to the importance of his maleness and its function in perpetuating patriarchal privilege.[14] That being so, I suggest that the focus on Jesus' forced nudity as a man serves as a threat to patriarchy, as the Son of God then becomes a victim of sexual violence. According to contemporary rape culture, Jesus is therefore exposed and emasculated, thereby rupturing expectations of hegemonic masculinity; and, as noted earlier, similar ideals of men are found in the time of the biblical writers. The fact that Jesus is covered up in representations of the crucifixion leads to an inability to recognise Jesus' sexual abuse, confronted as we are with images of his physical abuse and scars from his torture. The inability to recognise Jesus' sexual abuse, therefore, extends to sexual violence against men in general. Salient to my discussion here is that the stripping and exposure of Jesus does matter in order to engage in a robust critique of sexual violence against men, obfuscated through religion, as noted in Chapter 1. We are thus able to explore the content and relevancy of the biblical texts to today's world. The Bible upholds the masculine values of strength, dominance, and power demonstrated by men in the scriptures that give rise to contemporary ideals of men. The cherished conviction that maleness is privileged and divinely sanctioned has resulted in bias throughout Jewish and Christian scholarship, and is rightfully critiqued by feminist, womanist, queer, and intersectional approaches.

Textual violations?

Given the explicit focus of this book on sexual violence, it would be an omission not to include how the discussion in this chapter thus far may appear to run the risk of a textual violation by containing academic analysis that speculates on Jesus' nudity. Claims that such speculation is an act of semiotic rape need to be examined. J. Cheryl Exum is concerned with the objectification and violence that take place within biblical texts and examines the textual violations committed by biblical writers against women (2016 [1993]). In being drawn into this discussion, and encouraged to reflect on it, there is a need for further examination of Exum's points in relation to the passage of bathing Bathsheba. As noted in Chapter 2, the Bible is a man's text, where the (heterosexual) male readers of the text in 2 Samuel 11 are assumed. In *Fragmented Women*, Exum articulates feminist concerns about the portrayal of the scene where David is watching Bathsheba bathing, incisively observing

> we presume she is naked, or nearly so; at any rate, we are forced to think about it, to disrobe or partially robe her mentally. Is not this gaze a violation, an invasion of her person as well as her privacy?
> (2016 [1993]: 139)

Exum expresses her disquiet at the biblical text as follows: 'For my part, I am uncomfortable being put in the position of voyeur, watching a naked woman being watched' (2016 [1993]: 139). Feminist biblical criticism has made important and insightful critiques about the male gaze on women in the Bible, yet I am aware that the same criticisms can be levied at any scholarship focussing on Jesus' own nudity. Exum's concern about an invasion of person and privacy can be addressed towards representations of a nude Jesus. Yet the rarity and censorship at play in presenting a naked Jesus in art must be acknowledged here, nor is Jesus objectified. For clarity, my focus here is on how the humiliations of Jesus at the crucifixion are sexual, as well as physical. Shedding light on Jesus' own abuse in this way impacts on social and cultural perceptions of other male victims whose own sexual abuse is, like Jesus', often ignored or not seen. Moreover, choosing to ignore or failing to acknowledge Jesus' abuse or, indeed, any sexual abuse against men, only serves to perpetuate myths around sexual violence against men and contributes to further abuse through its silencing and hiddenness. Therefore, there is a tension between the actual biblical texts and traditional Christian thought as well as the presentation of the passion and crucifixion in the real world. My exploration of the relationship between the central story of Christianity, as described in readings of Jesus' own forced nudity through his stripping, serves to bridge the literary text with the real world and turn the focus to male victims. Indeed, the parallels between naked Bathsheba and naked Jesus are not so simple to draw, as positioning the male as the object of the gaze is outside of the heteronormative sphere, where the viewer, androcentrically, is assumed to be male, too.

In a move away from the androcentric gaze to address the problem of male–male focalisation, the position of Deryn Guest (2008) helps to find a liminal space between lesbian and feminist approaches. Guest reflects on the lesbian gaze in being presented at an academic conference with an image of a nude Bathsheba (2008). The image depicted Bathsheba sitting in a bath while two handmaidens washed her skin. It raised discomfort among the attendees, who raised questions of objectification and the 'racial exoticism represented by having a pair of dark hands involved in handling the naked white Bathsheba' (2008: 231). Guest's response was mixed, being fully conscious and cognisant of the feminist perspective, while unpicking her own personal response to the image from a lesbian perspective. Guest comments how a lesbian perspective can 'transgress a feminist taboo that women should not themselves sexually objectify another woman' (2008: 231). Heteronormative assumptions are also at play in feminist readings, an issue Guest begins to probe. It is not too difficult to compare Guest's experience and critique here with the idea that (heterosexual) men do not objectify men. Guest too echoes Exum's observation of voyeurism – namely, that eyes should be averted to avoid collusion in sexual objectification. Guest draws on Exum's position that Bathsheba is a literary creation, and therefore the rape is semiotic rather than physical.

Guest's critique offers two important points. First, it ruptures the presumed heterosexuality of the biblical characters; second, and most pertinent to my discussion here, the critique massages some of the tensions in relation to the gaze between subject and object. In laying feminist concerns to one side, Guest can appreciate the position of David, experiencing pleasure in the beauty that is before him. Guest sees this not as colluding in the male gaze, but offering a distinctive position: 'A lesbian gaze is not a male gaze and it does not objectify Bathsheba all over again. In fact, maybe it can, instead, spring her free from her entrapment to the male gaze' (2008: 239).

Guest posits that the lesbian reader/viewer may appreciate the view through David's eyes, but she is not trying to take his place. This would be abhorrent, as 'David's character represents a performance of masculinity that any self-respecting dyke would despise' (2008: 245). The lesbian gaze is respectful and less exploitative. While feminist critiques have examined and exposed patriarchy, Guest's critique examines and exposes heteronormativity, which, as noted in Chapter 1, is one of the foundations of hegemonic masculinity alongside patriarchy and misogyny.

In light of this discussion, attention now turns back to Jesus. Hegemonic masculinity functions through misogyny and homophobia, thereby setting out a clear set of rules in which men should not be feminised. In addition to objectifying women, the hegemonic male gaze operates to police masculine performativity, and any deviation from this has detrimental social consequences. The subtext is quite clear: men do not look at other men; men only look at women. Thus, men are unable to conceive of other men as victims. An attempt to extend this gaze to be able to recognise other male victims, including Jesus, breaks from hegemonic masculinity: it is disruptive and contravenes expectation. In order to preserve patriarchy and male privilege, such disruption is often met with resistance and ridicule. Yet, Guest's argument allows us to conceive of the plurality of experiences a gaze draws, rather than rely on simple assertions of a gaze always being exploitative and destructive. Just as Bathsheba can be freed from her entrapment under the male gaze, Jesus too can be freed from the silence and hiddenness of his sexual abuse. Breaking free from an abusive, heteronormative gaze, following Guest, allows men to set their eyes towards Jesus' abuse and removes the panic of homophobia as well as the chaotic fragility of hegemonic masculinity. Consequently, this allows men to see other men as vulnerable. This is of pivotal importance to draw the male gaze to recognise sexual abuse against men, given the cultural and social ignorance concerning male abuse.

Conclusion

Exum asks why biblical commentaries have described Bathsheba as a passive object of the scene, rather than a victim of rape. She asks: 'Can it be because most commentators are men, and men are uneasy accusing other men of rape, even in an ancient text?' (2016 [1993]: 137). Absolutely. And the same question can be posed about the sexual violence against Jesus at the crucifixion, as Jesus is stripped by other men in the gospel accounts. Moreover, the question can be extended even further to reflect men's attitudes to sexual violence against men: there is a move from a gaze to a total lack of perception. In the same way that sexual violence is about power rather than sexual desire, my exploration of Jesus' vulnerability as a man stripped nude is not about sexualising or objectifying him. It is about shedding more light on the religious, cultural, and social dynamics of sexual violence against men, punctuated as they are with patriarchy, homophobia, homonegativity, and toxic, hegemonic masculinity. In this sense, the act of not looking extends to a position of being blind to recognising sexual violence against men, as it is hidden in plain sight. While the reality of sexual violence exists in contemporary society, with 1 in 6 men reported to have had unwanted sexual experiences, very few men are still able to label it as sexual abuse. The concluding remarks that follow in the next chapter briefly consider the impact and issues of exploring religion, rape culture, and the Bible in public settings and in higher education.

Notes

1 I agree with Reaves and Tombs, who note the lack of attention given to Trainor's work. They state that 'given the very public debate which has taken place over church sexual abuses in Australia in recent years, it is extraordinary that Trainor's work has not received more attention. The silence with which the book has been received suggests a deep discomfort in discussion of the topic' (2019: 19–20).
2 In Exodus 28: 42, there is a clear stipulation that men are required to wear underwear – 'Make linen undergarments to cover their bare flesh, extending from waist to thigh' – while the consequences of failing to do so when approaching an altar or holy place include incurring guilt or death, as revealed in the next line.
3 For an examination of how Jesus' silence is connected to silence around sexual abuse, see Katie Edwards, 'I was Taught Silence was Strength. Then I Witnessed Sexual Assaults', *The Guardian*, 21 March 2018. Available: www.theguardian.com/commentisfree/2018/mar/21/silent-child-abuse-religion-rotherham-weinstein. See also Katie Edwards, 'The Silence of the Lamb', *BBC Radio 4 Lent Talks*, 2018. Available: www.youtube.com/watch?v=SEMODEdW6x0.
4 For further discussion on how Jesus' silence is problematic for victims of sexual violence, see Katie Edwards and Meredith Warren, '#MeToo Jesus: is Christ really a good model for victims of abuse?', *The Conversation*, 14 February 2018. Available: https://theconversation.com/metoo-jesus-is-christ-really-a-good-model-for-victims-of-abuse-91812.
5 Katie Edwards and David Tombs, '#HimToo – why Jesus should be Recognised as a Victim of Sexual Violence', *The Conversation*, 23 March 2018. Available: http://theconversation.com/himtoo-why-jesus-should-be-recognised-as-a-victim-of-sexual-violence-93677.
6 This chapter focusses on the accounts of Jesus' passion and crucifixion in the gospel accounts, and therefore an exploration of Jesus' ministry is beyond the scope of this book. However, for explorations of Jesus' masculinity and his inclusion of women, see Sara Parks, *Gender in the Rhetoric of Jesus: Women in Q* (Lexington Books, London, 2019) and the collection of essays edited by Stephen D. Moore and Janice Capel Anderson, *New Testament Masculinities* (SBL, Atlanta, 2003).

7 Some of the non-canonical gospels (i.e. the Gnostic gospels) depart from traditional interpretations of Jesus as celibate and unmarried. Speculation on Jesus' marriage, for example, is found in a papyrus fragment examined by Karen King (2014). The extract represents a dialogue between Jesus and his disciples in which Jesus speaks of 'my wife'. King notes that 'the fragment does not provide evidence that the historical Jesus was married but concerns an early Christian debate over whether women who are wives and mothers can be disciples of Jesus' (2014: 131). The fragment is entitled 'The Gospel of Jesus's Wife'. The fact that depictions such as these are either non-canonical or not accepted by mainstream denominations renders them fringe and subversive. The reaction, therefore, is very telling about mainstream Christian views on Jesus' sexuality. Also, Jesus is sexualised in a number of mystic texts, as sacred eroticism was a key feature of the vernacular languages used by medieval women to describe their unions between God and devotee in the mystics. See Amy Hollywood's chapter 'Queering the Beguines' (2007).
8 In the introduction to *Queer Theology: Rethinking the Western Body* (2007), Gerard Loughlin describes the wedding at Cana, reflecting on how John 2: 1–11 does not detail who got married, but that the story is loaded with double meaning. Loughlin suggests that Jesus is the bridegroom. According to Loughlin, Jesus was marrying his beloved disciples: 'a queer kind of marriage – the bonding of men in matrimony' (2007: 2).
9 Examples of this work are available: https://edwardknippers.com/.
10 It is worth noting how intentional nudity or exposure in UK law is covered by the Sexual Offences Act (2003). Section 66 of the act stipulates that a person convicted of the offence of intentional exposure holds a maximum sentence of two years in prison. The Office for National Statistics in the UK conflate 'indecent exposure' and 'unwanted sexual touching' in their recording of data. There is no clear rationale for the collapse of both offences, and both can provoke quite distinctive responses from victims. Indecent exposure or unwanted sexual touching (11.5% of adults aged 16 to 59, 3.8 million victims) was more common than rape or assault by penetration (including attempts) (3.4%, 1.1 million victims). Office for National Statistics, 'Sexual Offences, Appendix Tabs', 8 February 2018. Available: www.ons.gov.uk/peoplepopulationandcommunity/crimeandjustice/datasets/sexualoffencesappendixtables.
11 In a similar but less graphic example, Robert Beckford comments on the representation of the Maasai Christ; as he writes, 'the squatting position of the Christ means that his testicles are visible in the bottom of his robes. This is significant because the icon depicts Jesus as a black warrior and a black sexual being' (1996: 19). Beckford's work goes beyond notions of Jesus' sexuality to explore intersectional issues within representations of Christ in theology, with explicit connections to race and socio-political contexts. Beckford's central argument is that 'black theologians must engage in the production of images of Jesus that symbolize the quest for a *black socio-political sexual wholeness*' (1996: 10; Beckford's emphasis).
12 Althaus-Reid is concerned with the use of sex and sexuality in order to challenge dominant theologies. Elsewhere but related, Althaus-Reid asks, 'Is theology the art of putting your hands under the skirts of God?' (2004: 99). The metaphor of lifting one's skirt, according to Althaus-Reid, leads to an honest and critical self-reflection in the production of theology. She states: 'We start our reflections from our own sexual stories. We lift God's skirts after having lifted

our own first. In lifting our skirts we remind ourselves of our own identity at the moment of doing theology while we remain committed to theological honesty. It is from an alliance of sexual epistemologies in disagreement with heterosexual ideology and not vice versa that we reflect on grace, redemption and salvation' (2004: 107). Althaus-Reid also opens *Indecent Theology* with the call for the Argentinian woman theologian 'to remove her underwear to write theology with feminist honesty' (2000: 2). With specific attention to sexual violence, Sophie Witherstone observes how such a call is problematic for a woman who has experienced sexual abuse. Witherstone's demand is that real bodies are taken more seriously in the academy, especially sexually abused bodies, as this breaks the silence caused by abuse. This is significant for my focus on Jesus in this chapter as we consider what Jesus' abused body signifies for male victims of sexual abuse. Sophie Witherstone, 'Autoethnography: The Voice of a Sexually Abused Body', 24 May 2019. Available: https://shiloh-project.group.shef.ac.uk/autoethnography-the-voice-of-a-sexually-abused-body/.

13 Although her work was reputed for its shock and scandal, it may seem surprising that Althaus-Reid takes issue with Beckford's paper 'Does Jesus Have a Penis?' (1998), as she states, 'the "Jesus = Penis" discourse is part of a homophobic discourse, which homologises heterosexuality and normativity' (2000: 106). She continues, 'such an affirmation that "Jesus had a penis" is no more intriguing than affirming the presence of pubic hair in the women of the Gospels. It does not add to any critical discourse on the Gospel' (2000: 107). Althaus-Reid's critique focusses on sexuality and therefore does not engage directly with the point of Beckford's argument, which is more concerned with God-talk and its exclusionary effects on Black people. He remarks, 'We must seek to answer the question: "how can the images, icons and even language about God confront sexist, racist, classist and heterosexist representations of black people in popular culture"' (1996: 11).

14 Elsewhere, Althaus-Reid draws on the work of Judith Butler to note how the phallus is ubiquitous. She claims, 'it is precisely that phallus which represents the transcendental in theology – a phallus which depends on a messianic prototype, that is the prototype of the mystical penis of Christ' (2004: 100). She continues by noting how a subversion of the penis by feminist theologians is not an act of desire, but an act of pleasure, as feminist theologies offer 'antidotes to the unnecessary transcendence of the Father's phallus in Jesus and in God' (2004: 100).

References

Althaus-Reid, Marcella. 2000. *Indecent Theology*. London: Routledge.
Althaus-Reid, Marcella. 2004. 'Queer I Stand: Lifting the Skirts of God'. In *The Sexual Theologian*. Edited by Marcella Althaus-Reid and Lisa Isherwood. London: Continuum, pp. 99–109.
Beckford, Robert. 1996. 'Does Jesus Have a Penis? Black Male Sexual Representation and Christology'. *Theology & Sexuality*, 5: 10–21.
Caprioli, Sarah and David A. Crenshaw. 2017. 'The Culture of Silencing Child Victims of Sexual Abuse: Implications for Child Witnesses in Court'. *Journal of Humanistic Psychology*, 57/2: 190–209.
Eilberg-Schwartz, Howard. 1994. *God's Phallus and Other Problems for Men and Monotheism*. Boston: Beacon Press.

Exum, J. Cheryl. 2016 [1993]. *Fragmented Women: Feminist Subversions of Biblical Narratives*. Second Edition. London: Bloomsbury.
Finley, Stephen. 2007. 'Homoeroticism and the African-American Heterosexual Male: Quest for Meaning in the Black Church'. *Black Theology*, 53: 305–326.
Friedman, David M. 2001. *A Mind of Its Own. A Cultural History of the Penis*. New York: The Free Press.
Ganzevoort, Ruard R. 2001. 'Religion in Re-Writing the Story. Case Study of A Sexually Abused Man'. *International Journal for the Psychology of Religion*, 112: 45–62.
Ganzevoort, Ruard R. 2008. 'Scars and Stigmata. Trauma, Identity, and Theology'. *Practical Theology*, 1/1: 19–31.
Gross, Rita. 1983. 'Steps Toward a Feminine Imagery of Deity in Jewish Theology'. In *On Being a Jewish Feminist*. Edited by Susannah Heschel. New York: Schocken, pp. 234–247.
Guest, Deryn. 2008. 'Looking Lesbian at the Bathing Bathsheba'. *Biblical Interpretation*, 16: 227–262.
Heath, Elaine A. 2011. *We Were the Least of These. Reading the Bible with Survivors of Sexual Abuse*. Michigan: Brazos Press.
Hengel, Martin. 1977. *Crucifixion*. Philadelphia: Fortress Press.
Hollywood, Amy. 2007. 'Queering the Beguines: Mechthild of Magdeburg, Hadewijch of Anvers, Marguerite Porete'. In *Queer Theology: Rethinking the Western Body*. Edited by Gerard Loughlin. London: Blackwell, pp. 163–175.
Isherwood, Lisa. 2108. 'Sexuality and the "Person" of Christ'. In *Contemporary Theological Approaches to Sexuality*. Edited by Lisa Isherwood and Dirk von der Horst. London: Routledge, pp. 277–288.
Isherwood, Lisa and Dirk von der Horst. 2018. 'Normativity and Transgression'. In *Contemporary Theological Approaches to Sexuality*. Edited by Lisa Isherwood and Dirk von der Horst. London: Routledge, pp. 3–22.
Keener, Craig S. 2009. *The Gospel of Matthew: A Socio-Rhetorical Commentary*. Cambridge: William B. Eerdmans Publishing Co.
King, Karen L. 2014. '"Jesus said to them, 'My wife . . .'": A New Coptic Papyrus Fragment'. *Harvard Theological Review*, 1072: 131–159.
Kinsey, Alfred, Wardell Pomeroy and Clyde Martin. 1948. *Sexual Behavior in the Human Male*. Philadelphia: W.B. Saunders.
Kinsey, Alfred, Wardell Pomeroy, Clyde Martin and Paul Gebhard. 1953. *Sexual Behavior in the Human Female*. Philadelphia: W.B. Saunders.
Le Donne, Anthony. 2013. *The Wife of Jesus: Ancient Texts and Modern Scandals*. London: Oneworld Publications.
Loader, William. 2005. *Sexuality and the Jesus Tradition*. Michigan: Wm. B. Eerdmans Publishing Co.
Loughlin, Gerard. 2007. 'Introduction: The End of Sex'. In *Queer Theology: Rethinking the Western Body*. Edited by Gerard Loughlin. London: Blackwell, pp. 1–34.
Nelson, James B. 1979. *Embodiment*. Minneapolis: Augsburg Publishing House.
Phipps, William E. 1973. *The Sexuality of Jesus*. London: Harper & Row Publishers.
Reaves, Jayme R. and David Tombs. 2019. '#MeToo Jesus: Naming Jesus as a Victim of Sexual Abuse'. *International Journal of Public Theology*, 13: 1–26.

Reynoso, Rondall. 2013. 'That's Not Art . . . That's Nekkid: Edward Knippers and the Aesthetic of Nudity in Evangelical Christianity'. Available: www.academia.edu/4051817/That_s_not_Art_That_s_Nekkid_Edward_Knippers_and_the_Aesthetic_of_Nudity_in_Evangelical_Christianity.

Romano, Elisa and Rayleen V. De Luca. 2001. 'Male Sexual Abuse: A Review of Effects, Abuse Characteristics, and Links with Later Psychological Functioning'. *Aggression and Violent Behavior*, 6: 55–78.

Satlow, Michael L. 2001. *Jewish Marriage in Antiquity*. Princeton: Princeton University Press.

Steinberg, Leo. 1996 [1983]. *The Sexuality of Christ in Renaissance Art and in Modern Oblivion*. Chicago: University of Chicago Press.

Stephens, Elizabeth. 2007. 'The Spectacularized Penis Contemporary Representations of the Phallic Male Body'. *Men and Masculinities*, 101: 85–98.

Stiebert, Johanna. 2016. 'The Voice of God in the Hebrew Bible'. *Journal for Religion, Film and Media*, 21: 23–32.

Tombs, David. 2018 [1999]. 'Crucifixion, State Terror, and Sexual Abuse'. *Union Seminary Quarterly Review*, 53: 89–108. Available: http://hdl.handle.net/10523/6067. Republished as David Tombs. 2018. *Crucifixion, State Terror, and Sexual Abuse: Text and Context*. Dunedin: University of Otago, Centre for Theology and Public Issues, 2018. OUR archive http://hdl.handle.net/10523/8558.

Trainor, Michael. 2014. *The Body of Jesus and Sexual Abuse. How the Gospel Passion Narratives Inform a Pastoral Response*. Eugene: Wipf and Stock.

Trible, Phyllis. 1984. *Texts of Terror: Literary-Feminist Readings of Biblical Narratives*. Philadelphia: Fortress Press.

Afterword

The simple aim of this book was to shed light on how patriarchy, heteronormativity, and misogyny are integral to hegemonic masculinity, and how this serves to obfuscate sexual violence against men. Moreover, I have argued that religion also has a role to play in this through my exploration of biblical texts. Hegemonic masculinity keeps sexual violence against men hidden and silenced. The societal ideologies of patriarchy, heteronormativity, and misogyny function to regulate masculinities, and a male victim of sexual assault, therefore, threatens the hegemony of male power and patriarchy. As a result, many male victims fail to report their assault. Sexual violence against boys and men therefore remains a social, cultural, legal, and religious issue that urgently needs addressing. And while there is a growing awareness of this issue, much more work needs to be done.

Despite this increased awareness, unhealthy and unrealistic expectations of men and masculinity still remain in society and culture. The examples of sexual violence against men highlighted in this book demonstrate how myths around male victims of sexual violence have endured from ancient contexts to the present day. In order to be fully 'masculine', men and boys are taught to avoid showing their emotions, to be strong and powerful, to be penetrators. Indeed, men are designated as penetrators exclusively in religious teaching about sexuality, where the purpose of sexual activity should equate to procreation. In reality, however, such ideals of masculinity are harmful to masculine identities. The practical task that lies ahead for us is to continue with the dismantling of ideologies and practices that continue to be harmful.

The interdisciplinary exploration of contemporary social and cultural attitudes towards sexual violence against men and the biblical texts documented in this book may prove to be challenging reading for some individuals. If the critical discussion in this book has caused shock, outrage, and disgust, we must acknowledge that these are among the same emotions experienced by victims of sexual violence. If we try to hide the stories of sexual violence against men in the Bible or explain them away as belonging to ancient cultures or contexts, we hide the victims and place a silence on them, too. That silence has reigned for far too long.

Exploring rape culture and violence may offer a contemporary lens to studies in religion, theology, or biblical studies in today's market of higher education. Yet the research and teaching of such topics do not exist in a university vacuum separated from the reality of sexual violence. Deryn Guest reminds us of the import and function of the Bible in today's world, noting how we cannot compare biblical studies to the study of other ancient texts:

> We cannot imagine that our teaching of biblical texts exists in some kind of objective, detached way from these controversies. When we run modules on biblical ethics, the contemporary interpretation of biblical texts, the Bible in the modern world, the Bible and the ancient world, or whatever, we are not dealing with ancient texts that are on a par with those of, say, Plato or Herodotus. We are dealing with texts that are absolutely fundamental for religious institutions and which provide ammunition for policymaking in both church/synagogue and state.
>
> (2012: 163)

Guest goes on to note how the most important concern for us is how the texts affect the lives of students and other citizens.[1] Those of us who research and teach about rape culture and the Bible are acutely aware of the range of sensibilities and sensitivities needed to create a safe, comfortable environment for students. Rhiannon Graybill describes how this is imperative given the prolificity of sexual abuse:

> I used to take a certain glee in revealing to students the nastiness of the Bible, its many narratives of horror, revulsion, or simple ickiness. But given the prevalence of sexual violence, including rape, on college campuses, I no longer draw any pleasure from bringing this particular strain of biblical nastiness to light. Instead, I am increasingly concerned with the problem of teaching these texts to students who have experienced sexual violence firsthand.[2]

There is an ethical imperative, therefore, that we do not risk traumatising students by discussing the Bible as if its contents were abstract and belong specifically to ancient eras and contexts. Ethically, we must exercise caution and ensure that students' engagement with such a sensitive and polemical topic is informed and consensual. Yet, this process involves activities that sustain critical thinking and reflection, as teaching, learning, and researching about sexual violence across a variety of disciplinary contexts is activism.

Exploring sexual violence and the Bible allows us to engage with stories that have been shrouded in stigma and shame; we are lifting the silence on voices that have been muted, and we place in plain sight what has been obscured.

Notes

1 Guest is not engaging explicitly with the theme of sexual violence here. The concern expressed here relates to the actual lives of LGBTI students and citizens.
2 Graybill, Rhiannon. 'Teaching about Sexual Violence in the Hebrew Bible', *Oxford Biblical Studies Online*. Available: https://global.oup.com/obso/focus/focus_on_sexual_violence/.

Reference

Guest, Deryn. 2012. *Beyond Feminist Biblical Studies*. Sheffield: Sheffield Phoenix Press.

Index of biblical passages

Hebrew Bible

Genesis
  1:28, 71
  2:25, 37
  3:7, 37
  3:10, 37
  6:4, 48
  9, 49
  9:1, 58n6, 71
  9:7, 58n6, 71
  9:20–27, 5, 35, 47–49
  9:21, 47
  9:22, 47
  9:23, 47
  9:24, 47
  9:25–27, 47
  16, 43
  19, 23, 47
  19:1–3, 45
  19:1–29, 5, 9, 21–22, 23, 30n26, 35, 41, 44–47
  19:4, 45
  19:5, 45, 48
  19:6, 46
  19:6–7, 45
  19:8, 40, 45
  19:9, 45
  19:10, 45
  19:11, 45
  19:12–15, 45
  19:16–17, 45
  19:18–23, 45
  19:24–25, 23, 45, 48
  19:26, 45
  19:27–28, 45
  19:30–38, 5, 35, 39–41
  19:33, 39
  19:35, 39
  20, 41
  24:2–9, 37
  34, 68
  34:2, 58n10
  37:23, 39
  39, 5, 41–44
  39:4–6, 41
  39:6, 43
  39:9–11, 42
  39:14, 42
  47:29, 37
Exodus
  28:42, 82n2
Leviticus
  18:7, 49
  18:22, 24
  20:11, 58n6
Deuteronomy
  21:23, 63
Judges
  3:12, 49
  3:12–30, 5, 35, 49–51
  3:14, 49
  3:15, 49
  3:16, 49
  3:17, 49
  3:19, 49

3:21, 49
3:22, 49
3:24, 49
3:25, 49
4, 5, 35, 51–52
4:9, 51
4:18–19, 51
4:20, 51
4:21, 51, 52
5, 52
5:24–27, 52
9:54, 37
13, 52–53
13:1–5, 53
13:5, 53
13–16, 52
14:19, 39
16, 5, 35, 52–55
16:4–5, 53
16:5, 53
16:6, 53
16:7–14, 53
16:16, 53
16:17, 53
16:19, 53
16:20, 53
16:21, 54
16:25, 54
19, 5, 9, 30n26, 35, 44–47
19:1–2, 45
19:4–10, 45
19:11–21, 45
19–21, 30n26
19:22, 46
19:23, 46
19:24, 46, 58n10
19:26, 46
19:27, 46
19:29, 46
20, 46
20:5, 58n10
1 Samuel
  18:7, 39
  31:3–5, 37
  31:9, 37
2 Samuel
  6:14, 37
  6:22, 38

10:3–4, 39
11, 79
11:15–18, 41
13, 68
13:12, 58n10
13:14, 58n10
13:22, 58n10
13:32, 58n10
1 Kings
  12:10, 38
Job
  30:11, 55
  30:14, 55
  30:15–16, 56
  30:17–19, 56
  31:10, 54
Isaiah
  20:2–4, 38
  41:2, 54
Jeremiah
  2:23–5:19, 71
  13:22, 56
  20:7, 56
Lamentations
  1:8–10, 39
  3, 39
  5:11, 58n10
Ezekiel
  16, 71

New Testament

Matthew
  1:18–23, 73
  1:25, 73
  5:28, 57n3
  21:12–13, 36
  23:12, 64
  26:65, 63
  27:28, 63
  27:31, 63
  27:35, 63
Mark
  11:15–18, 36
  15:5, 64
  15:17, 63
  15:20, 63

Luke
  2:21, 70, 75
  2:41–51, 73
  14:26, 36, 74, 78
  23:9, 64
  23:11, 63
John
  2:1–11, 83
  3:29, 71
  19:1–2, 63
  19:5, 62–68
  19:23, 63
1 Corinthians
  6;19–20, 57n3
  7:8, 71
  16:13, 19
Ephesians
  5:21, 71
  5:22, 29n17
Colossians
  3:5–14, 57n3
1 Timothy
  2:9–10, 57n3
1 Peter
  3:3–4, 57n3

Index of authors and subjects

Abdullah-Khan, Noreen 15
Abraham 37, 41, 43
Adam 37, 75
alcohol 39–40, 57n4
Althaus-Reid, Marcella 64, 78, 83n12, 84n13, 84n14
Ammonites 39, 40–41
arousal 13–14, 41, 57n2; *see also* erection

Bal, Mieke 52, 58n9
Barton, John 2
Bassett, Frederick W. 58n7
Bathsheba 41, 42, 79, 80–81
BDSM 55
Beckford, Robert 72, 83n11
Bergsma, John 48, 58n6
Berra, Robert 20
Bible: Hebrew 34–57; importance of 2; as male book 35–36; toxic masculinity in 4; violence in 2
Blyth, Caroline 2, 3, 4, 59n12
Boyarin, Daniel 24
Burgess, Ann 10
Burke, Tarana 16
Butler, Judith 84n14

Canaan 5, 37, 47–49
Canter, David 10
Caprioli, Sarah 64, 65
#ChurchToo 18–20, 29n17, 29n19, 30n20
clergy 18–19, 29n17, 30n20, 66
Clines, David 2, 35–36, 57n2
Colgan, Emily 3

Connell, Raewyn 8
consent: arousal and 13–14, 41; in definition of rape 9–10; of Jesus 69; of Joseph 42; of Noah 48; of Samson 55
Conway, Colleen 24
Coxell, Adrian 12, 16
Crenshaw, James 56, 64
crucifixion 62–64, 73, 74, 75, 76, 78, 79, 80, 81, 82n6
culture, rape 1, 20, 22, 40, 44, 46, 69, 78, 82, 88

David 36, 37, 38, 39, 41, 81
Deborah 51, 52
Delilah 5, 52–55
Derks, Marco 54, 58n11
Deurloo, Karel 40
Dinah 2, 68
disempowerment 14, 62, 65, 77

Edwards, Katie 3, 4, 30n22, 65
Eglon 5, 35, 49–51
Ehud 5, 35, 49–51
Eilberg-Schwartz, Howard 48, 71, 72, 77–78
ejaculation 13, 14, 15, 41
Embodiment (Nelson) 70
erection 13–15, 41, 54, 75, 78
Eve 37
Exum, J. Cheryl 2, 5, 46, 47, 79, 80

female rape 2–3, 11, 14, 16, 36–37
feminism 2, 79, 80
Fewell, Danna Nolan 51, 52
Finley, Stephen 71

foreskin 75
Fragmented Women (Exum) 79
Friedman, David 75
Fuchs, Esther 40

gang rape 30n26, 44–47
Ganzevoort, Ruard 68
gay men: as demonised 9; Genesis and 21–23; homophobia and 20–21; impact of rape and sexual abuse on 15; marginalisation of 8, 36; sexual identification of, after assault 15; sexual violence as associated with 1; as victims 10, 28n10; *see also* homophobia
Gelfer, Joseph 19–20
Gibeah 45–46
Gibeahite 30n26
God's Phallus and Other Problems for Men and Monotheism (Eilberg-Schwartz) 77–78
Graham, Ruth 11
Gravett, Sandie 53, 54, 55–56
Graybill, Rhiannon 38, 88
Greenberg, Stephen 24, 31n28
Greene, Mark 12, 14
grooming 51–52, 56, 58n8
Gross, Rita 72
Groth, A. Nicholas 10
Guest, Deryn 30n22, 49–50, 80–81, 88
Gunn, David 51, 52
gym culture 19

Hagar 43
Hahn, Scott 48, 58n6
hair 53–54
Ham 5, 35, 47–49, 58n6
Hanun 39
Harding, James 47
Heath, Elaine 64
Hebrew Bible 34–57
hegemonic masculinity 11, 12, 19, 35–39, 43, 55–57, 64, 66, 69, 71, 74, 77, 78, 81, 82, 87
Hengel, Martin 63
heteronormativity 25, 26, 45, 47, 59n12, 78, 80, 81, 87; *see also* homophobia
Hodge, Samantha 10
Hollander, Jocelyn 25, 26, 27

homophobia 11, 20–21, 23, 24–27, 71; *see also* gay men; heteronormativity
homosexuality *see* gay men
hooks, bell 12
Hornsby, Teresa 40–41
humiliation 5, 14, 24, 27, 28n8

incarnation 73
incest 40, 41, 48, 49, 58n6
India 17
Isaiah 38
Isherwood, Lisa 70, 75
Israelites 40–41

Jacob, Benno 40
Jael 5, 51–52
Japheth 47
Javaid, Aliraza 10, 11, 14
Jesus: crucifixion of 62–64, 73, 74, 75, 76, 78, 79, 80, 81, 82n6; as married 74–75, 83n7; nudity of 62–82; penis of 75–79, 84n13; purity of 72–73; sexuality of 70–75, 83n7, 83n11; violence of 36
#JesusToo 68–70
Job 55–56
Jonathan 50
Joseph (New Testament) 73
Joseph (Hebrew Bible) 5, 35, 37, 39, 41–44
Joy, Emily 18
Judaism 31n28
Judas 67

Keener, Craig 65
Kessler, Martin 40
King, Karen 83n7
King, Michael 12, 16
Knippers, Ed 72

Loader, William 74
Long, Ronald 3
Lot 21, 35, 39–41
Lot's daughters 5, 21–23, 35, 39–41, 44, 45–46, 47, 48, 58n6, 58n9

man box culture 12
Man of Sorrows (van Heemskerck) 76
marriage 74–75, 83n7
Mary 73

masculinity: of God 77; hegemonic 11, 12, 19, 35–39, 43, 55–57, 64, 66, 69, 71, 74, 77, 78, 81, 82, 87; male rape and 11; performative 19–20; and 'real men' 12–13; religious imagery and 30n22; silence and 11; toxic 4, 19, 20, 25, 26, 37, 69; victimisation and 12–13; *see also* patriarchy
men: 'real' 12–13; suicide among 28n12; *see also* gay men; masculinity; patriarchy
#MenToo 16–18
metaphorical sexual violence 47–56
#MeToo 2–3, 16, 19, 27, 29n16, 30n20
Michal 38, 39
microaggressions 12, 21
militarism 30n22
misogyny 5, 22, 24–27, 69, 74, 81
Moabites 40–41
Moses 24
myths, about sexual violence against men 1–2, 8–27

nationalism 30n22
Nelson, James 70, 73
Niditch, Susan 53–54
Noah 5, 35, 47–49, 58n6
nudity 37–39, 48, 57n3, 62–82

orgasm 14

Paasch, Hannah 18
Pascoe, C. J. 25, 27
patriarchy 25–26, 37, 45, 46, 66, 69, 74, 77, 78, 81, 82; *see also* masculinity
patriotism 30n22
Paul 19, 36, 71
penetration 9–10, 24, 26–27, 28n5, 34–35, 40, 46, 50–52
penis 28n5, 41, 75–79, 84n13, 84n14; *see also* erection; foreskin
performative masculinity 19–20
Peter 67
Phillips, Anthony 49
Phipps, William 73–74
Pilate, Pontius 63
Pirson, Ron 43

Index of authors and subjects 95

post-traumatic stress disorder (PTSD) 8, 15
Potiphar's wife 5, 35, 41–44, 57n1
purity 20, 72–73
Purnell, David 17–18

rape culture 1, 20, 22, 40, 44, 46, 69, 78, 82, 88
rape, female 2–3, 11, 14, 16, 36–37
rape, male: criminalisation of 28n2; defined 9–12; gang 30n26, 44–47; impact of 15–16; masculinity and 11; men in 10–11; penetration in 9–10; shame and 12–15; statistics 10; stigma and 12–15; women in 9–10
'real men' 12–13
Reaves, Jayme 66, 67, 82n1
Rehoboam 38
reporting 10, 12–13, 14–15, 20, 28n6, 87
Retief, C. Wynand 58n6

Samson 5, 52–55
Sarai 43
Satlow, Michael 57n3, 74
Saul 37, 39
Scholz, Susanne 42, 43, 49–50
Sedgwick, Eve Kosofsky 25
Seifert, Elke 41
Sex Offences Act 9, 83n10
sexual abuse: in church 66–67; defined 4, 9–12; impact of 15–16; metaphorical 47–56; reporting of 10, 12–13, 14–15, 20, 28n6, 87
sexuality: hair and 53–54; of Jesus 70–75, 83n7, 83n11; male 13–14, 30n22, 77; wine and 48
shame 12–15, 24, 27, 37, 75–76
Sharon, Diane 58n9
Shem 47
silence 11, 18–19, 29n17, 64–66
Sisera 5, 35, 51–52
Sivakumaran, Sandesh 10–11
Sodom and Gomorrah 5, 21, 22, 40, 41, 44–47
Sodomite 30n26
sports 19, 28n8, 30n22
Steinberg, Leo 75, 76

Stephens, Elizabeth 77
Stiebert, Johanna 3, 43, 44, 57n1, 58n10, 72
stigma 12–15, 20, 23, 24–27, 51–52, 63, 65–68
suicide 13, 15–16, 28n12, 37

Tamar 68
terminology 4
Thorsen, Jens Jorgen 70
Toensing, Holly Joan 23
Tombs, David 65, 66, 67, 82n1
toxic masculinity 4, 19, 20, 25, 26, 37, 69
Trainor, Michael 63, 64, 69, 82n1
trauma 16, 26, 68; *see also* post-traumatic stress disorder (PTSD)
Trible, Phyllis 2

van Heemskerck, Maerten 76
victimisation, masculinity and 12–13

von der Horst, Dirk 75
von Rad, Gerhard 49

warriors 19
Waters, Sonia 22, 30n26
Weiss, Karen 12, 15
Westboro Baptist Church 20–21
wine 48
Witherstone, Sophie 84n12
womanlessness 36–37
women: in Bible 2; in India 17; and male gaze 81; nudity of 65; as perpetrators 1–2, 9–10, 40–43; Sodom and Gomorrah story and 22–23; as victims 10, 28n8; *see also* female rape; feminism; #MeToo; misogyny; rape, female; *specific female figures*

Yahweh 36, 71
Yee, Gale 52

For Product Safety Concerns and Information please contact our EU representative GPSR@taylorandfrancis.com
Taylor & Francis Verlag GmbH, Kaufingerstraße 24, 80331 München, Germany

www.ingramcontent.com/pod-product-compliance
Lightning Source LLC
Chambersburg PA
CBHW051103230426
43667CB00013B/2430